The King's Man

The Urban Guide for Reborn Men

By L. William Martin

TABLE OF CONTENTS

Acknowledgments

I would like say thank you to God for being my inspiration, my knowledge and my light. Thank you to my mother, Lucille and my father, Randolph for giving me a chance to be on this earth. I would also like to thank my children, Roshon, Kiesha, and Rodney for showing me that I am not the only important person. I also appreciate my ex-wives for showing me how to act and how to not act. Thank you to my brother Steve who showed me that I had artistic value. Thank you to my sister Elvira who showed me that I had an intelligent side. Thank you to my sisters Rosalee and Liz who taught me never to give up. Thank you to my brother of another mother, Rodney, who puts up with me no matter what I do. To Judges E. Michael Kaiser and Judge Victor Miceli, two of the most noblest men I have ever known. To Pastor Jim, my inspiration. And a special thanks to my wife, Ellen, who steadily gives me the support, and love I need on a daily basis. May God bless and keep you all!

THE KINGSMAN

PREFACE

The purpose of this book is to align newly devoted men with the word of God and to allow boys to become men in Christianity. Many men go down the center aisle of their church when the pastor calls for people to commit or recommit themselves to God. You are probably one of those who were tired of life as it existed before you went to church that morning. Or maybe you were inspired by the pastor or another Christian. Or maybe you were a church-goer at one time before and you simply wanted to come back to the church.

Walking down the center aisle to accept Jesus as your Lord and Savior comes with responsibility. It is not enough for men to call themselves Christian. We, as men of God have to learn how to walk the Christian way of walking. We have to talk the Christian way of talking. We have to learn how to exude Christianity and we must be able to teach it to our children. However, I hope that by writing this book, sectarians as well as women may also be able to benefit from this. This book is certainly not the beginning and the end of the Christian learning experience. There are many more experienced persons out there who can educate and motivate people far better than I. And I encourage the new Christian to continue reading and listening to these scholars, pastors, prophets and apostles. However, I also ask you to read them and listen to them with care. Do not take what one person says and adopt it as your sole reference. Keep in mind that one book is only one person's opinion of what they have read and understood.

While reading this book, keep in mind that I am only expressing my interpretations of Christianity and what you should do to become a good Christian.

4

Also keep in mind that Christianity is and always has been a process. We truly do not become instant Christians simply by joining a church or becoming baptized or praying each day. Yet some of us call ourselves Christians after taking one or all of these steps only to succumb to the many exploits of worldly living. We continue gambling. We continue using profanity. We continue smoking. We continue abusing our families. Ideally, Christianity is not only a belief that Christ died on the cross for, but it is a lifestyle of peace and joy.

Some of us join a church and only attend Easter and Christmas services. Some of us don't pray each day. After what we are lacking in our Christian walk is brought to our attention, there are promises that are made to others and ourselves that we seldom keep. There are promises of true repentance, the promises of forgiveness, and of being more Christ-like. All are promises we make to ourselves and sometimes to others. But somewhere along the way we lose them in the familiarity and comfort of our everyday selves. We lose the commitment. We lose the enthusiasm.

Believe me, I understand too well how you have been feeling. My past is full of episodes of ungodly living and broken promises. Which gets me to the next point.

Yes, my earlier life has not been one of an upstanding citizen. I have been married a couple of times, I shot up heroine, I robbed people. There was even a woman in my life that I slapped around a couple of times. I have done all of these things and more that I am truly ashamed. However because my God is a forgiving God and because he is a God of second chances, he has allowed for me to use my experience to write this book for you as well as allow this essay to be my own therapeutic experience.

THE KINGSMAN

Perhaps you would like to hear that I was a Christian since I was nine years old and that I was the good child in my family of three sisters and one brother. But in reality, I was not. And If you would really like to hear from someone who is either inexperienced in worldly affairs or a good guesser, then it would be best that you put this book down immediately and walk away from it.

Would not you like to hear from someone who has had bad experiences just like you may have had in your life and has been able to overcome obstacle after obstacle with the grace of a loving God. Isn't it better to get advice from someone who has actually been through the storm rather than from someone who has never felt a raindrop or a snowflake or a hale ball hit their bare head. After all, how could it be possible for a person thoroughly encapsulated in a protective rubber suit be able to describe how rain or snow or hale really feels. In actuality, they would say that rain looks wet, but they would not be absolutely sure. Snow looks cold, but they would wonder. Hale looks hard, but they would marvel. And they would not be able to give you definite answers about the characteristics of either.

Another point I would like to make in this book is that in order to get clean and sober, I had gone through an 'anonymous' group. I had also attended church on a regular basis during my earlier sobriety. As an aside, I truly believe that anonymous groups and churches need to come closer together for addiction recovery. I was able to use the church and the anonymous group to keep me sober, even though each organization has different theories about the other. And generally either rarely flatters the other.

A persons language is very important. Our characteristics are part of our profile. You know what is said about first impressions. A person's first impression is not only

6

your hygiene and the clothes you wear, or our smile, but, it also is the language you use. If your character is an arrogant cussing sailor, then that is the profile you project. Believe me. I understand that you may be having a bad day. But once the person you are meeting has the impression of who they think you are, it is very difficult for you to live it down.

Children are extremely important in a man's maturity. If you have any, they must be respected throughout the maturity of both of you. You must love them no matter what they or you do or what they or you say. Because you are the adult, it is natural that you are the leader in this relationship. And to do that you must lead them to be Kings men and Kings women and show them how to take their proper place beside the thrown of our Christ. And if you are the child, you must be able to look past your own wants and desires and be a good follower until it is your time to lead.

Relationships sometimes come and go. And I am not going to tell you to remain in a relationship with your wife if you are totally miserable and see nothing else to do but placing a bullet between your teeth or putting your head in an oven. All I am saying is that God wants us to be happy. Don't initiate any of the bad behavior that is common amongst many men. Bad relationships usually leads to bad behavior by all parties involved. Though it must be tough, you must be an example to your spouse or significant other...an example of exemplary behavior. If this is difficult, then perhaps you should not be in a relationship anyway. However if you want to stay in a relationship, you have to figure out a way to be a better person. One way to do it is to keep God in your mind and in your heart all times.

Honesty is another subject that will be looked at in this book. Being less than honest can only get us life in a pit of fire.

Remember that you are a Christian to obtain one goal. It is to be a Kings Man. Being a King's Man means that you are a follower of Christ who has a destiny of being a prince in Heaven. Biblically speaking, you will sit at the footstool at the thrown of Jesus. You went to the altar to emphasize, to yourself and others, your purpose. So know I will tell you how to obtain and maintain your righteousness.

I would like to close this preface with some clichés. 'We are only human.' 'Take it one day at a time.' And, 'Let Go and Let God!' Even though I do not particularly like using clichés, these are a few my favorites that reflect the theme of my everyday thinking. But I have to always remember first and foremost to make 'God first in my life'. Whoops another cliché.

Now let's get going with what you are reading for!

Chapter One
SURRENDER

Proverbs 3:5-6

Trust in the Lord with all your heart, and do not lean on your own understanding. In all your ways acknowledge him, and he will make straight your paths.

1 Corinthians 10:13

No temptation has overtaken you that is not common to man. God is faithful, and he will not let you be tempted beyond your ability, but with the temptation he will also provide the way of escape, that you may be able to endure it.

Romans 12:1

I appeal to you therefore, brothers, by the mercies of God, to present your bodies as a living sacrifice, holy and acceptable to God, which is your spiritual worship.

If you watch old movies, surrendering means fighting until you can't fight any more. It means giving up to someone you were trying to prove that was inferior. It means taking out that white flag and waiving it and subjecting yourself to a power who you once thought was inferior. You will surrender to a greater power that is likely to put you in shackles... to incarcerate you in a prison... feed you what they want to feed you... and make you do what you do not ordinarily want to do. It has been ingrained in our minds that surrendering never has a good ending.

God is a power more greater than any man can ever subject you to. But when it comes to surrendering to God it means subjecting yourself to a greater power... A magnificent power... A mighty power... A glorious power. Surrendering to God means that our every need will be met. He will not shackle you nor put you in a prison. He actually frees you. He frees you from sin. He frees you from adulterous ways. He frees you from lying. He frees you from stealing. He frees you from addiction. He frees you from cheating. He frees you from all the negativity in your life. Mind you, negativity comes in your life no matter who you are. However, with God in your life you know that the future will be handled by Him because he does not want anything or anyone to harm you for you are chosen by Him.

James 4:8

Draw near to God, and he will draw near to you. Cleanse your hands, you sinners, and purify your hearts, you double-minded.

Surrendering is not easy. It requires humility. When you realize that you are about to be overtaken by a power greater than yourself, it requires you to bow down, so to speak. There is a king that now resides in your heart and because of it you must realize you are weaker than the King. You have to admit that you can no longer exist without his leadership. And most of all, you must believe in Him. If you do this, you will be gentler, kinder and joyous. The greatest burden you bear will become less burdensome because you will now know how to share your pain with God.

Have you ever gone through periods in your life when things go so bad you don't think they could get any worse. Then all of a sudden, they do? Perhaps you suddenly had gotten behind with your mortgage payments. Your child is bugging you because they want to go on a field trip that you cannot afford. Your wife is bugging you because the gas bill is late. Your boss is bugging you because you are late on a project. You find that life is becoming so awful. You're getting pressure from all sides. It cannot get any worse. Or can it? Then out of the blue, you receive a pink slip at work and your wife leaves you, and you get into a car accident on the way home. Indeed your problems may be different than the examples I just gave, but, I am sure you understand what I am talking about. You don't want to give up. So you do what you have been taught to do. You fall to your knees.

Or how about this for an example? When you have children that will not listen to you. And they would not do their homework. And they want to listen to rap or punk rock music with their explicit lyrics...and they want to hang out all night long... and they talk back to you... And just when you thought it could not get any worse, You get a call from the police. They tell you that your kid has been arrested for assault. Once again, you fall down to your knees. Do you surrender?

Or when you go to the hospital because you think you have the flu. You have been down for a week. You're throwing up, you have a fever, you have chills going through your body, your heart is racing. You have to be helped out of the car to get to urgent care. Just when you think it could not get any worse, the doctor diagnoses you with cancer. So now, you summon your strength to build a prayer closet. You fall down to your knees. Do you surrender and ask God to deliver you from your misery?

Sometimes we take matters in our own hands. We do whatever it takes to make it right. Some has gone so far as to sell drugs or rob banks, prostitution, burglaries and some have become violent. Some have beaten their children or sent them to military camp. Some have started taking all kinds of herbal supplements. But all we have to do is call on Jesus. Jesus has a way of leading us to what is necessary in our lives. Call on Jesus because he will lead you to make rightful decisions. And in some cases, he will instruct you to wait. But in the end, He will straighten out every crooked road. He will give us peace at tumultuous times. But in order for him to do this you have to surrender. We have to truly surrender. We have to give our all. We cannot just pray to God until things get better, like so many of us do. We have to make choices that are different and in line with God's demands.

Use your conscience rather than your body's ability to react to situations. Your conscience is a direct link to the Holy Spirit. It is your conscience that assists you to make correct choices.

When you surrender, you have to be able to tell God that you cannot do life anymore without help from him. Tell him to take over. Let him know that you will not interfere with what his intentions are. And you will not make any decisions without speaking to him first. This will be a very difficult task since most of us have lived most of our adult lives making our own decisions, being self motivated and being reactionary. However, after you surrender, you can make your own decisions but with God's guidance. God encourages us to make our own decisions. Jesus encourages us to make good decisions to stay within God's grace.

Try going into your private place, lift up your hands and say I SURRENDER! I SURRENDER! I SURRENDER! Confess your sins. Perhaps your sin is something that you may not be aware of. Maybe your sin is the way you communicate. Maybe your sin is your swagger at inappropriate times. What we may consider as little sins matter to God. And it may be the little things that you are doing why God is allowing you to suffer now.

My point here is we have to be aware of what we are doing wrong before we can correct it. Let's say, for example, that when you speak you have a habit of cursing. You may come off as someone who is aggressive or mean-spirited. You may not realize it but you are putting some people off. If you work in an environment where everybody cusses and uses profanity and you take this language home with you, your family will take this as you're being aggressive. You don't realize it. However, your children pick up on this aggressive behavior. Your wife, who is trying to go to church regularly, grows weary of it. Yet you go on talking the way you do because it has been ingrained into you by your work environment.

So when you pray at night, you ask God for forgiveness of your sins and for clarity. Then you start cussing at your children before God has a chance to smile at you. We must be aware of how others see ourselves, but what is more important, is how God sees us.

Try this. Ask for God to allow you to see yourself as other people see you. Then go to a friend who is non-judgmental and will keep your conversation in private. A church mentor or a pastor would be the ideal person if you are unable to trust a friend. Tell him that you are just trying to see yourself as others see you. Explain what it is you are going through. Be honest and tell him you want him to be honest. Then ask him, how you can make changes in your life that would better yourself.

Whatever you are told by your mentor or pastor, you must lovingly meditate on. Turn the television off (in total silence) and think about what they have told you for about 15 minutes a day for about one week.

Now you are ready to surrender. Give whatever is bothering you to God. And work on making yourself a better person. Keep God in your heart and on your mind at all times.

By implication, keeping God in your heart and on your mind at all times is constant work. Just think that God is wonderful. Imagine, if you will, God's wonderful work. Everything you look at should remind you of God. When you look at the trees, imagine His wonderful work. When you look at your children, don't look at them as another mouth to feed. Imagine them as His wonderful creation. When you look at your wife or girlfriend, don't look at her as someone to argue with. Imagine that God has placed this wonderful love in your life. When you look at your boss and your friends, don't look at them as people you have to tolerate. Imagine God is wanting you to take on their positive traits and leave behind the negative.

When you do this you surrender the negatives of the world and accept the positive energy of the Holy Spirit. You begin to accept things and attitudes as they are and look at things more positively rather than accepting them as negative connotations, attitudes or actions.

The bible is full of stories of people who surrendered.

Exodus 14 tells us the story of Moses and how he led the Israelites away from slavery in Egypt. Their destination was on the other side of the Red Sea. God had instructed Moses to take the long way around and so Moses did as God told him. All the way, the former slaves moaned and groaned. They were tired and weary. They finally arrived at the Red Sea and found they had nowhere to go as they stood before the waters. They had mountains to the left and right of them. Pharaoh and his army was closing in from behind. The people feared the position they were in. The Israelites were starting to go against Moses. They spoke against God and Moses' interpretation of what God had been telling him. Moses told them to "Fear Not, stand Still and see the salvation of the Lord." Moses continued to tell them, "The Lord shall fight for you, and Ye shall hold your peace." You know what happened. The people of Israel surrendered to the will of God. And they were delivered from Pharaoh's wrath.

Depending on which commentary you read, the people of Israel were ready to surrender to Pharaoh. And if they had, there would not have been the story of one of God's greatest miracles. He parted the red sea and allowed the Israelites to cross on dry ground. And in the process God had destroyed Pharaoh's army.

If the Israelites were to turn around and had surrendered to Pharaoh's army they would have gone back into slavery. Isn't this sometimes what we do? We take the easy way out. We turn around and go back to what we are used to even though we know that it is not the right thing to do.

How many people do we know that have been incarcerated, and when they are released, they pray to God for a better way of life. Instead of waiting for the blessing, they decide that it is time to get high or to stick up one more person, or to sell one more bag of meth. Patience is a key. Patience and works. We will talk about works later in this book.

And you better be careful who you surrender to. If you surrender to sin, you will end up in eternal damnation. If you do not surrender to God's will you will find yourself in bondage, like the Israelites would have been if they turned around and submitted themselves to Pharaoh. Discernment is a biblical way of the ability to differentiate evil from Godly.

Looking at your situation today, you may be surrendering to fame and fortune, or to lust, or to money, or to pride. It may look good, feel good, sound good, and smell good but, much of these distractions are not of God. What's more are the truths that these things will take you to eternal damnation. In your walk with Christianity you will learn that before Christianity, the things that look good, feel good, sound good, and smell good are not the same as what looks good, feel good, sound good, and smell good after Christianity. And this is a good thing. You can still be happy. As a matter of fact, you will be much happier. You will no longer have to worry about what lies ahead of you. You don't have to worry about being found out that you are a crook, or an adulterer, or an intravenous drug user, because you will no longer be those things. And, what's more is that no one has to know what you were because God also knows how to keep secrets. It is people who cannot keep their mouths shut.

The book of Jonah tells us that Jonah was a priest who knew God, yet he refused to obey the will of God. God gave Jonah a job to do. Jonah did not want to do it, so he surrendered to his own will. He stowed away on a ship in order to hide from God. But God is so all knowing, so vast, so all encompassing. God knew just where Jonah was. He made it so the ship Jonah was in was engulfed by a terrible storm. Jonah knew the storm was the wrath of God. He had the shipmates throw him overboard in order to save the ship and the ship's crew. As soon as he was thrown off the ship a large fish engulfed him and swallowed him. While in the belly of the large fish, Jonah was angry. God sustained Jonah in the belly of the large fish for three days. Jonah prayed. And finally he surrendered to a God that he knew that was more powerful than him. He was delivered on dry land and went to Nineveh, as per the instructions given to him by God, to warn its people of God's wrath.

There are many of us who know the law of God yet they are embattled by evil every day and like, Jonah, we submit to our own will. Have you ever hung out with someone you know that your wife would not approve. It gets later in the day or evening. You know that it is time to go home, but for some reason, you hang out longer and longer. You don't think about the vows that were made on your wedding day. Remember? You promised to love and honor! But your actions show neither. You finally go home to an unhappy wife. She does not wait up for you and goes to sleep before you come home. And if she did wait up, she would have been able to smell the alcohol on your breath or the perfume on your clothes or the marijuana beneath your fingernails. It would have certainly turned into a vicious argument. And sure enough, you feel guilty. If you were a Christian you would have known that what you have done, whether it be being out with the boys, or hanging out at the bar, or innocently being in the company of another lady, coming home at a late hour was inexcusable and not a Godly thing to do. And sure enough the guilt would have set in some time before you laid your dizzy head on the pillow.

You would have realized somewhere along the line, also, that you had to make repentance. You would have to say you are sorry to your wife and you would have had to confess to God of your sins. This is what Jonah went through. He did not want to obey the will of God because he did not want to tell the people of Ninevah that God had a message for them. You did not want to obey the vows that you swore before God and witnesses. God put Jonah in a position that he had to think about his transgression. He also put your wife to sleep to give you time to think about your own transgressions. He brought on a guilt to Jonah so that he was forced to repent. And he does the same to you.

Don't get me wrong, repentance is a choice. Will you repent? I do not know. Will you submit to the will of God? I do not know. Will you surrender your will to the will of God. I do not know. But you must try. Repentance is the only way one can live in peace and to rid yourself of the guilt. Otherwise, metaphorically speaking, you will always live in the belly of a large fish.

And then there is Job. (Pronounced Jobe). You know the story of Job. He was a rich man by any standard during his time. He had servants, he had cattle, he had children, he had real estate and he had crops. Then all of a sudden, they were all gone. The devil took them all. And just when Job didn't think it could get any worse, the devil struck Job with leprosy. Job had friends come to see him who insisted that Job had made God angry. But Job refused to think that God was the one who cursed him with this bad fortune. And if it was God, there was good reason. His wife suggested that he Curse God and Die!

Job was a faithful man, a patient man. He had a choice. To curse God or to Surrender to God's will. What did he do? He continued to worship God. He continued to pray. He continued to have an undying faith. He surrendered! He Surrendered! He Surrendered! He gave his will to God. He was continuously in prayer. And as the story goes, God gave to Job many times what he had before.

This goes back to what I said earlier about having things going wrong in your life and just when you think it couldn't get any worse, it does. However, the story of Job also gives us another valuable lesson. And that is that men of God must be patient.

Are you a nit-picking husband or stern father or a stubborn friend? Are you very rigid in your thinking? Are you impatient when other people are not doing or saying things "correctly" or to your liking? Job had his closest people, his wife and his friends, giving him advice about ways to deal with what had happened to him. Most thought that Job's misfortune was what God had chosen for him to punish him. Actually, God chose Job to show the world and the devil that faith (in Him) conquers all iniquities.

So, Job would not allow himself to think that his wife's and his friends' opinions were correct. He did not argue with them. He did not shove them out of his door. He did not kick the dog. He simply prayed. You see, Job had a faith in God that can be determined as being immeasurable considering the situation he was in. Job spoke to God. And God did answer.

So whenever you think that things cannot get any worse, don't argue, just seek out God. Seek peace by placing yourself in the loving arms of God. Pray. Know that he is going to answer your prayers. Surrender yourself to the will of God.

Now look at these examples I gave you. Moses, Jonah and Job. They all got the victory.
One thing you can be assured of is that God is the only being you can surrender to and get the victory at the same time.

Some people are more concerned with appearances rather than being concerned about what goes on in the inside of themselves. Scripture says, and I am paraphrasing, that we cannot be overly concerned about works. That is, we should not measure our achievements on earth and expect that to be our key to the entrance into heaven. All of us want to have nice things. We want up-to-date cars. We want big houses. We want nice clothes. But we should be more concerned with what is on the inside of us. One way a person is measured on the inside is the way they speak... the way they communicate with others. This is very important because the minute we open our mouths, someone draws a conclusion of you. Someone is determining, where you are from, how much education do you have, your ethnicity, are you really a Christian? The way you speak and the things you say are reflections of your heart.

The One thing that bothers me more than anything is the language of people who call themselves Christian. That is our people. We are living in a time where we hear profanity like it is generally accepted in the world and in some Christian homes. Some of us think because we are not in church that we can use any language we want. We can escape God's wrath because we can hide in our house or in our car. Because the pastor's not looking or hearing us we can say what we mean and mean what we say and say it any way we choose. Yet we still call ourselves Christian. I would like to remind you that when you call yourself a Christian you represent a vast nation (nearly one third of the earth's population). You represent the Father, the Son and the Holy Spirit. And to people who do not know the Father, the Son and the Holy Spirit, you are acting just like one of them. And perhaps you use the language you use because you want to look like or feel like one of them. But, I am telling you, you can't be one of them and a Christian too. It's too late now for you to go back and claim a heathen life by the language you use. If you are a Christian, you know too much and you cannot go back. Surrender your tongue to God.

Your tongue is more powerful than a sword. Therefore, be mindful of what you say and how you say it. What you say can cause someone to commit suicide. Your tongue can cause someone to want to fight you or someone else, your tongue can start a war, your tongue can get you placed in jail. As well, your tongue can make someone feel good about others and themselves. Your tongue can cause peace. Your tongue can also cause someone to come to Christ.

The book of Isaiah tells us of how the Lord was looking for someone to speak on his behalf. God wanted to warn the children of Israel that they had better straighten up. Isaiah wanted to do it but he declared he had "unclean lips". So God sent an angel to Isaiah and purged his lips with a hot coal. When God asked again, who will represent us, Isaiah replied, "Here am I, Send Me."

When God had asked for a volunteer to speak for him and Isaiah told him that he had unclean lips, God did not say, "that's cool." Go ahead and talk, represent me with that filthy mouth of yours. No! He cleansed the mouth of Isaiah with a hot coal first. Now I ask you, do you think God wants you representing Him with that filthy mouth you have. Oh, I know I am talking to someone out there. You may be a reader who is feeling uncomfortable right about now! You have got to surrender yourself to God. You have got to submit yourself to the hot coal. You have to surrender. A cleansed mouth is the only way God wants you to represent him.

Matthew 16:24-27

[24] Then said Jesus unto his disciples, If any man will come after me, let him deny himself, and take up his cross, and follow me.

[25] For whosoever will save his life shall lose it: and whosoever will lose his life for my sake shall find it.

[26] For what is a man profited, if he shall gain the whole world, and lose his own soul? or what shall a man give in exchange for his soul?

[27] For the Son of man shall come in the glory of his Father with his angels; and then he shall reward every man according to his works.

From this scripture, Matt 16:24-27, there are three things you have to do in order to surrender:

1. Recognize
2. Develop humility
3. Give your all

First, you have to recognize there is a problem. It's easy to recognize when the children don't behave, or when there is no money when the bills are due. It's easy to recognize when you are physically ill.

However, most people also have trouble recognizing their own shortcomings or character defects, if you will. They go through life acting like a horse's rear end and actually think that they are cool. They live life oblivious to the feelings or emotions of others. Some of us beat-up other people emotionally. Some of us talk about people behind their backs. Some of us turn our noses up on people who have less than what we have. We act like we are better Christians than someone else because we quote scripture more easily than others. The ones that do not have think that the ones that do have, think that they are better than they are. These are sometimes subtle attitudes we portray, however it may be glaring to some. What I am saying is Recognize that there is a problem. Being a new Christian means it is time for self-recognition. It is time for self-identification. It is time for self-examination.

And, don't ignore the feedback! I heard the following at a meeting for Narcotics Anonymous.

If someone calls you a horse's rear end, you might ignore it.

If a second person calls you a horse's rear end, you might want to turn around to see if you are growing a tail.

And if a third person calls you a horse's rear end, you might as well slap on a saddle.

Recognize that you have a problem or character defect that is less than Godly. Work on it or them! Whether it be impatience, poor language, meanness, stubbornness, whatever! Recognize them and do something about them.

I find that if you surrender yourself to God, he will show you a way to deliver yourself from your shortcomings.

You are right, "No one is perfect". Perfection is not obtainable, however we, as Christians, should always strive for perfection. Know that you will never get there in this lifetime, but we have to put forth the effort. Our hearts are always revealed to God. And if we are not trying to be better persons on earth, then our hearts are not into making improvements. Do you think that God wants someone in heaven who didn't even try on earth?

Second, developing Humility:

The definition of Humility is, the state or quality of being humble, marked by meekness or modesty in behavior, attitude, or spirit; not arrogant or prideful.

1 Peter 5:5

Likewise, ye younger, submit yourselves unto the elder. Yea, all of you be subject one to another, and be clothed with humility: for God resisteth the proud, and giveth grace to the humble.

God does NOT abide in you if you are displaying ego or "proud-ness". Give in to God. After you have done all of the proud things… after you discover that it is your ego that gets you into trouble, know that it is time to get God back in you. Give in to the power of God. Let him do what he promised to do. And I promise you He will make every crooked road straight. Stop stumbling on your pride.

Get out the way! Let God be the magnificent wonder that you know he can be. Stop getting in the way with your own ego and your pride. Bow down. Bring out that white handkerchief. Show him that you are putting your ego aside. Keep your mouth shut and be still for a change.

1 Peter5:5 is speaking to younger people who think that they know more than an older person, however this scripture should be accepted by all.

I know of a man who has a daughter. In her teen years she would not listen to him or accept his guidance. She would not do her homework. She had poor school attendance. She wanted to hang out where she wanted to hang out and come home when she wanted to. The more this father butt heads with her, the more she butted back. She wanted to talk to her mother any old kind of way. She was beating on her little brother. He argued with her. He took away her electronics. He begged her. There came a time when the father decided that his approach was not working. He asked God for guidance. He asked God for His help. As he asked, the calmer he became. He became calmer because he allowed the Holy Spirit to come into his life. And God worked what some people would call a miracle. As the father became calmer, so did his daughter became calmer. And he noticed that she started coming home earlier. And, she started going to school. And her grades were getting better. She stopped hanging out.

Oh children, you don't know what you're up against when your parents team up with God against you and that devil. You don't have a chance! When your parents start praying, and falling on their knees, their kids end up doing things you don't want to do. They get A's and B's on their report card and they wonder, "Where did that come from?"

Many times when parenting we know that we think we are supposed to have all of the answers. We get rigid in our disciplinary ways. If our pride is hurt by our children, we set ourselves on a routine disciplinary course. You lay down the rules and this is the way it is going to be. Then the children become teenagers and your rules are no longer working. You have forgotten that flexibility is an asset you have and your teenagers have not yet acquired. But your pride will not allow you to change your course. At this point you are ready to pull your hair out. Don't! Pulling your hair out is painful. Pray! Surrender! Submit your will to Him.

Note to children: When your parents submit to the will of God, you are a beneficiary. Your parents surrender to God and God sees to it that you submit to His will. You come home early, you wash the dishes, you take out the trash... You make a determination that you will do better.... And you don't know why? Yet you realize that you are doing the right thing. You are doing these things solely because it is the answer to your parents' prayers.

And sometimes it does not happen right away. Sometimes God wants you to go through a little (or in some cases a lot) more of whatever it is you are going through.

Sometimes God may wait until you become an adult before he restores you to righteousness. God may want to prepare you to deliver His message to someone who had never received the blessings of good Christian parenting, so He will wait until the time is right to bless you. God may want you to go through the drug addiction, or the alcoholism. He may want you to go through the prostitution. He may want you to remain incarcerated. And he wants you to come back from your dark journey to explain to the people, who never had God in their lives, about Him and how far He has brought you. So He will wait. What he has done in essence was to humble you in order to make you a better person. He molds you into submission. If you do not submit to him you may become bitter or angry. You may lash out at people who are close to you. You may become a doubter. You may become a hater. And God will wait some more. God is in control, not you. And he will let you know this by making you wait some more. You will have to live in your own misery until God is satisfied that you have humbled yourself.

In Luke 15 Jesus tells us about the Prodigal Son. The Prodigal Son wanted to go off by himself to have some fun. So he asked his father for the inheritance he would have received if after his father's death. He gave it to him. The Prodigal Son then went off to a land far away and started to party. He probably had as many women as he could. He probably gambled. He probably drank and did drugs. Then he found himself surrounded by famine. His money ran out. He took on a job caring for pigs. He then found himself sleeping with the pigs. He found himself eating with the pigs. His living and eating arrangements were a far cry from the comforts of his father's house. The Prodigal Son was humbled to nothing. Some people would say he was at rock bottom. Others would say he was lower than the curb he had been kicked to. He decided to go back to his father who received him with open arms.

One lesson we get from this parable is that sometimes, we have to become humble in order to accept God and Christ in our lives. His father recognized that humility and accepted him back into his home. So does God recognize the humility and accepts us.

And third. When you surrender you have to give your all. Jesus told his disciples in Matthew 16:24, *If any man will come after me, let him deny himself, and take up his cross, and follow me.*

When you surrender, you gotta come with it! There are no half-steppers in heaven and God expects you to be no different. You have to put everything aside that is not of God. You got to stay in his presence. Always moving closer to him. You must be willing to sacrifice what you want and accept what God wants for you.

Once you cross that threshold there is no going back. Because you have the knowledge, you have the tools, you know what it is like to have the taste of holiness in your mouth. You know what being in the devil's grip feels like and you don't ever really want to go back. You're willing to give everything you have in order to get into the graces of a mighty God. You must surrender every day. Give whatever it is to Jesus, who died for you. Who voluntarily went to Calvary.

He was tried. He was beaten. He was humiliated. They forced a crown of thorns on His head. His hands were nailed to the cross. His feet were nailed to the cross. He was cut in his side. Blood poured from his head hands and feet.

And after all that He said, "Forgive them for they know not what they do".

And there were two thieves who died beside him. One was forgiven. And that one was caught up.

It didn't matter what the thief had done in the past. He was caught up to heaven because at the end of his life here on earth, he humbled himself and surrendered. He declared Jesus as his Lord and Savior.

Don't wait until you are being crucified before you surrender. You will never know when you might get hit by a train, airplane or stray bullet or you may even be stricken with a massive heart attack. You can fall asleep after being poisoned. There may not be enough time for you to consciously surrender your life to Jesus.

John 3:16 says, *For God so loved the world that he gave his only begotten son, that whosoever believeth in him should not perish, but have everlasting life.*

It is clear in this scripture that God wants you to believe in Him and His son (Jesus Christ), so that he can give you everlasting life. This would mean that, if you believe in His son, you must believe in whatever Jesus said in the bible. And if you believe in what Jesus had spoken, you must believe that He has surrendered to the will of God. And if he has surrendered to the will of God, then you must also surrender to the will of God. Do it now! And do it forever!

Chapter two

LEAVING YOUR PAST IN YOUR PAST

The bible instructs us to leave all things in the past.

1 Corinthians 13:11
When I was a child, I spoke as a child. I understood as a child, I thought as a child; but when I became a man, I put away childish things.

Isaiah 43: 18
Remember ye not the former things, neither consider the things of old.

Paul's teaching in the book of Corinthians is one of the most highly quoted scriptures in the bible. On the surface it looks like Paul is telling us not to be a child when in actuality you are an adult. Let's look a little further.

If you look at Paul's teaching as I do, you might see something a little deeper. When you were a child, you did childish things. You spit up on yourself. You defecated your pants. You cried when you were hungry. All of which would undoubtedly be embarrassing behavior if you did that today. As you grew older, you played with toy cars, you believed in Santa Claus, and you may have even gone through a spell of bedwetting. Still a little embarrassing if you have the same behavior as an adult. Then when you got into high school, you may have started drinking, toying with girls' emotions, and using profanity. Now the line is no longer a line. The line gets blurry because there are many adults that still display the same behavior as they did in high school. Maybe it is you that have these behaviors.

What we have to do is make that line more distinct... bring the line into focus. You know that it is childish to spit up on yourself or to defecate your pants, or cry when you are hungry, but you have not realized that it may also be childish also to drink excessively, or toy with ladies emotions or to use profanity. Are you doing the same things you were doing 20 years ago?

As Christians we have to be able to distinguish what is childish and what is not. Did you pick up habits as a teenager that you are still addicted to today? Are they negative behaviors? Then they could be construed as childish behaviors that can have a negative impact on your spiritual adult self. Some examples of childish behaviors are, seeking attention, drinking excessively, drug usage, the use of profanity, general meanness, jealousy, smoking, lust, sexual deviancy, pity seeking, and many, many more.

When we are children we want to be noticed. We constantly fight for the love and affection of our mothers, fathers or guardians. If there are siblings, we are constantly competing for the attention of our parents. Sometimes we act out negatively because we long for our parents to acknowledge us. In our later years we may even conclude that a parent loves a sibling more than us. This places a burden on the family to show more affection to you than they would anyone else in the family which puts a strain on the psyche of your other siblings. It also places a burden on your parents. But the strategy works. So you go with it. Unfortunately you hold on to this strategy way into your adult life. Most of us men, will not admit it, but many times we are jealous when our wives or girlfriends go out with a friend to a movie or a dinner, and we are not invited. So our minds go into overdrive. Some of us become enraged enough to start imagining things that our wives or girlfriends are doing while they are out. We conclude that we are not loved. This behavior parallels with your longing of love and affection as a child.

Another example is the drinking and smoking of pot that you started at age fifteen or sixteen. Many of us have experimented with pot or alcohol at a young age. Some time along the way we realize that you have to stop. Some of us never do. Either your doctor tells you have to quit or die; or a judge tells you to quit or go to jail. Or maybe your wife tells you to quit or lose her. The doctor, the judge and the wife realize that the addictive behavior you are displaying is childlike. You are not making adult choices when you drink too much and wrap a car around a tree. Or that when you smoke too much pot, and all you do is lay around the house, eat and play video games. The doctor is concerned about your beer belly and your liver, but you don't care because you are living for the moment... much like children do! The judge is concerned about the welfare of the community. His lecture is very clear to you, but when you are released from custody, you are ready to go at all over again. More drinking and more smoking. Your wife is concerned about the safety of the family. You may argue about it all the time, but you are so entrenched in your position, like a stubborn child, that you don't even care if you are wrong or you are right. All you know is that you are going to win the argument.

Another example of childish behavior is the use of profanity. Some of us come from families where profanity was used all the time. We hear profanity used as everyday language. F.. this! F.. that! I am going to kick your a... Why the f... did this happen! S...!

It is amazing to me what we as a society have done to the English language. I was in the parking lot of a local supermarket. I was getting out of my car when three ladies and their shopping cart approached the car that was parked next to me. They appeared to be three generations. A grandmother, a daughter and a teenage granddaughter. The grandmother and daughter stopped behind their car to place the groceries in the trunk. The granddaughter went around to the passenger door and opened the door. "Mom", she exclaimed! "You forgot to lock the door." The mom replied. "No I did not. I know I locked the door." The granddaughter persisted. "Yes, you did." "How do you think I was able to get this door open?" As she stood there with the door open and looking at her mother. Instead of saying something that I would have expected a mother to say in front of her child and her mother... something like "Oh, my". Or "I made a mistake." Or even, "Check to see if anything is missing." She said M....r F.....r!

Do you think that granddaughter will be cussing for the rest of her life? In this case, it is obvious that, cussing is a way of life for the family. Cussing devalues the English language as well as cheapens any image one may have of the one doing the cussing. Cussing makes us look immature.

I remember, my mother rarely cursed when I was coming up. She was widowed when I was only eight years old. She would occasionally say the S word but usually it was used in humor. I do not recall her ever saying a cuss word out of anger. She attended church regularly and had her own ministry of visiting the sick and shut-in.

Back in the sixties when I was a child in Harlem New York, there was a man who lived across the street from us. We will call him Mr. Fay. Mr. Fay was generally eccentric and sometimes crazy. He was generally social, meaning that he would come out and hang out on the stoops... laugh and talk with the neighbors and that sort of thing. We all lived in tenement buildings. It was a hot blistery summer day. There were a lot of people on the stoops and milling around the area trying to catch a cool breeze from the Hudson River. Mr. Fay decided to come down stairs and outside the door with nothing on but his skivvies. Once on the stoop, he took off his underwear and proceeded to wave his wanger, laughing out loud. My mother was on the stoop across the street with her friends and neighbors. Some of the ladies laughed and turned their heads. The men were belly laughing so hard they did not see my mother march over across the street. She commenced to verbally rip Mr. Fay up one side, down another. She gave him a lasting tongue lashing I am sure he never had forgotten. She made him feel so small (no pun intended) all over. I believe she actually scared him back to his sanity. And she did not use one cuss word. He apologized to my mother, put on his skivvies, went back to his apartment, and did not come out of his house for weeks after that incident.

I am saying this to say that the tongue is a mighty and powerful weapon. We do not have to emphasize its strength by using inappropriate language. The tongue is mighty all by itself.

Once again, let us revisit Isaiah 6th chapter. It tells of a story when God was looking for Isaiah to prophecy throughout the nation and to warn the people of Israel that there will be consequences for their rebellion against God. Isaiah told God that he was undone because he was a man of "unclean lips". Isaiah was a holy man but he had a drawback. He cussed a lot is what I get from this scripture. Perhaps he considered his unclean lips to mean that he was cynical or maybe he was ornery and outspoken. But just for the sake of argument, let's say that he used a lot of profanity. At this point, God could have given him his assignment to go out to the nation and tell the people of God's displeasure, regardless of Isaiah's unclean lips. God could have said, "well maybe because everyone else has unclean lips, they will listen to you". Or maybe God could have said, "Go on out there anyway and deliver my message with that filthy mouth of yours". But no! God sent a seraphim (angel) to cleanse the mouth of Isaiah with a hot coal. This is telling me that God does not want us to spread his word with unclean lips.

Some of us clean up on Sunday, use the proper language while in the church. Observe the rules of the church while in the church. Have proper etiquette while in the church. Even go through the motions of speaking tongues, dancing down the aisles, tensing our bodies, shaking rattling and rolling, while in the church. We may do all these things on Sunday. But after Sunday comes Monday. And on Monday we commence to being our own regular worldly selves. The unclean lips reappear, the cynicism comes out like pouring water, the orneriness shows its ugly head. How can we be Christian and still display this ugly, ugly behavior? Do we really expect for someone to believe that we are the chosen people if we have unclean lips?

It's a matter of being believable. Could Isaiah have completed his task if he continued to have a filthy mouth and claimed that he was a messenger from God. Would anyone have believed him?

Does anyone believe you when you say that you are a Christian and you behave poorly amongst your family, your friends or your working associates. And more importantly, does God believe you?

Once you realize that cursing and cussing and carrying on is not the portrait you want to paint of yourself, then you should stop cursing and cussing and carrying on. Whenever a curse word slips through your lips tell yourself that you will do better. Apologize, not only to the person you cursed to or at (even if the word was in jest), but apologize to God. Ask him to forgive you. Then you must make a conscious objective not do it again

Remember that Paul instructed his student in *2 Timothy 2:16:*

But shun profane and vain babblings: for they will increase unto more ungodliness.

No matter. It is up to you now to change yourself. You are trying to become a new you. This is why you are reading this. If you want to leave your past in your past, perhaps you should also look at the language that you use.

Being believable is something that we all struggle with. We tell stories of our sordid past, which seems incredible to some people. You tell the stories and sometimes the story changes. You forget who you told the story to so you find yourself repeating the same story to the same person. Only this time the story changes. Does this make you believable? The simple answer to this is no! The person you told the story to catches something different in the story. He may continue to smile at you but, whenever you tell him any story the next time, he may view you differently.

Are you punishing yourself for your past? This is a problem that lies in the minds of most drug addicts who no longer use drugs, people who have had problems with anger and violence who have become humble, and criminals who become good citizens. What we tend to do when we were generally called the "dregs" of society and become good citizens is we overcompensate for what we were.

People, in general, should always be looking to do things better. Christians should look forward to each day with God's blessings… to expect God's mercy when we make a mistake… and to receive God's favor when we do well. From this we sometimes tend to do is to be too nice. And this is also common in the secular world. We allow our children to act badly more than we were allowed to 'act out' when you were their age. Sometimes, your children get you to back off of disciplinary procedures by reminding you how bad a parent you used to be. They do not want you to forget what you use to be and are actively using that against you. What you are doing is allowing some person from not allowing you to leave your past in your past.

Adults do this to other adults also. I once knew a person who we will call Tim. Tim became friends with this lady. They decided that they were going to be honest and open about everything in their lives. Tim was not use to this type of relationship. He was more use to holding his past in his past and whatever his mate found out about his past he would deal with it at that time. He would not withhold any information, he just did not choose to reveal his past all at once.

Anyway, Tim's girlfriend, who we will call Alice wanted to know everything about Tim. She wanted to know every feeling he had. She wanted to know about every girlfriend he had. How he felt about drug usage. How he felt about drinking.

THE KINGSMAN

Did he ever beat a woman? Did he ever masturbate? And every time they started talking about something in regards to Tim's past, she'd want to know more details. Tim relented most of his secrets to Alice. Further into their relationship, when an issue would come up between them, Alice would bring up Tim's past or what he freely told her about during their many conversations. Needless to say, Tim felt betrayed.

There is no way you can let your past be in your past if you are surrounded by a force that does not allow you to do just that.

Then there are friends who you used to drink beer with and chase the ladies with. And they would never let you forget the time you did something so stupid or so over the top that you wish you could forget it. What comes to my old mind is getting drunk at the office party. Our younger generation may think of something like untying a g-string off of a stripper before she was ready and being thrown out of the strip club. You may laugh and whoop at it even. However, now you should realize how demoralizing that may have been to the stripper. After all, she was groped by a total stranger. And then, it probably really was embarrassing for you. After all, how many people manage to be thrown out of a strip club? Anyway, if you are still hanging out with these friends who will not allow you to forget your sordid past and you are looking for a better, cleaner, more Christian way of life, perhaps you do not need these friends.

I have been told, and it is true, that whatever we have done throughout our young lives, it affects us throughout our adult life. Let's say that your parents were alcoholics or drug addicts. Perhaps they just smoked marijuana in front of you. Or maybe when you were sixteen or younger, your parents allowed you to smoke weed and or drink alcohol in the house. Be very careful in your adult life. You are going to be a person who thinks that you are entitled to privileges. However, when you are not granted those privileges you will become sorry for yourself. And when we feel sorry for ourselves we attempt to get sympathy from others. You may even now have the personality that no one really wants to be associated with because you are constantly trying to solicit sympathy. And your friends have been drained of all the pity they have been willing to give.

Then there are those who wish they had better "things" because they had been so impoverished when they were growing up. All is good when you look for a better and brighter future. But you must be careful what you aspire to be. You may become such the zealot that you become a worshiper of "things" rather than a worshiper of God.

What I am trying to get across to you is that you should leave your past in your past. Carrying your past with you all the time is self destructive. Look at yourself. Are you constantly soliciting sympathy? Do you talk a lot about "things" that you have in your possession? Are you constantly trying to solicit an emotion from another person... emotions that will boost your own ego or emotions of agreement to your situation? If the answer is yes, you are still the six year old that is always crying out "Mine" to his siblings or the eight year old that is constantly seeking the attention of his mother. .

It is time for you to realize that what you have done in your past has a lot to do with who you are today, however, God has a plan for you to succeed in a mighty way. And your success lies in your future, not your past. You cannot possibly succeed if your past is always with you in the forefront of your mind. Stop punishing yourself for being a bad person. Look around to the majority of the congregation of your church. Everybody has a past. Ask them. Ask your pastor if he has a past, but don't ask him the details if he does not volunteer them.

Discipline your children as you should. Do not allow your children to bully you because Child Protective Services came to take them away or you were not around when they were growing up. Each of these things will give you feelings of guilt, however, you must not the guilt rule your mind. And don't be angry your children either; rather, be disappointed. Remember that your goal is to remain a Christian and to raise your children as the same. Look ahead towards an earthly future as well as a heavenly revelation. Teach your children that the future is what they should look towards, especially if their past stinks. So that they too, should learn to put their past in the past.

As for the friends who are always bringing up the stupid things you have done in the past, you are going to have to let them know, in kind words, to leave your past out of their conversation. The best way to do this is to let them know some way, somehow, that you are now a Christian. If you stop cursing in front of them, they will hear you. If you do not get angry with them, they will feel the gentleness in your voice. If you drink lemonade rather than the alcohol, they will taste it. Over all, they will respect you. And do not waiver.

Put away your toys. Put away your childish behaviors and habits. As a child, there has always been someone to pick them up behind you but this time it is you who has to clean up behind yourself. Do so in an adult manner.

But, you may have to leave your friends behind. Your friends who drink, curse, get angry, and are violent, are a part of your past. You must make it clear who you are now, and you must leave them behind. They will not to speak to you as you speak to them. If you were to continue to hang out with them they will constantly offer you drinks and weed. They will constantly try to ware your faith down. They will always remember how you use to be. And they will not allow you to forget it. Actually, you will remember how you use to be by just by looking at them. Put yourself in a position where you will not have to look at them so often and you will not have to be reminded of your past.

Find some good people. In spite of what some people say about back-biting church people, most church members are good people. Seek out the members who are knowledgeable about scripture and appear to be walking the walk and talking the talk. Be leery of those who talk about others. Also, be careful of those who only go to Sunday Church Service and volunteer for nothing.

Also be careful of those people who wear Christianity on their sleeve. These are people who are always talking about how good God is and how good they are because they have been saved. They memorize scripture. These people generally look at every one else as wretches if they are not of their religious persuasion or denomination or do not believe precisely as they do. You can easily recognize these people because they will readily and easily give their opinion on just about everything. And don't tell them a secret unless you want it known. They may keep your secret for a little while, but if you do or say anything that may be construed as incorrect, all of a sudden others will be whispering behind your back because the secret got out.

Remember, that God is a forgiving God. Jesus brought the New Testament into being. He said that God loves us no matter what you have done in the past. Jesus made a blind beggar to see. He made fishermen into apostles. He forgave a man on the cross that was sentenced to die for his indiscretions. But most of all, He forgave a wretch, like me.

Forgiveness is letting go of transgressions against you that have taken place in the past. Therefore it is fitting to place Forgiveness in this chapter of Leaving Your Past in Your Past. Forgiveness is an art. It is something that is taught and then perfected throughout the life.

For example, if you leave two toddlers in a room with one toy. It is natural that the one who does not have the toy would be jealous of the one who does. The one who does not have the toy would go to grab the toy and the one who has the toy would instinctively rebuff the other. A fight may ensue. The parents intervene and teaches the art of sharing to the toddlers. The parents will also, more than likely, give the toddlers another toy to play with. Most of the time, afterwards, the toddlers get along and sometimes they may even trade the toys between themselves. This is an early lesson on forgiveness.

Then as teenagers, we get into physical fights with a friend or our sibling. No more than a week later we are all friends again, behaving like nothing ever happened.

I remember getting into a physical altercation with a great friend of mine because of something that was done or said. Our friends broke up the fight almost immediately because they knew of the brotherly bond that was between us. The next day we made up and took a trip to Coney Island together. Everything was forgiven. All was forgotten. In fact today we have been friends for more than fifty years. We call each other brothers.

However, later in life something happens to many of us. Once we are wronged by a friend or a family member we tend to hold grudges or resentments towards that person. There are some who do not care to forgive. There are others who do not know how to forgive. As adults we should take a more serious look at the bible and what it says about forgiveness. All throughout scripture we are told to forgive. Here are just a few examples.

Colossians 3:13
Bear with each other and forgive whatever grievances you may have against one another. Forgive as the Lord forgave you.

Matthew 8:21-22
Then Peter came to Jesus and asked, "Lord, how many times shall I forgive my brother when he sins against me? Up to seven times?" Jesus answered, "I tell you, not seven times, but seventy-seven times.

Luke 6:37
Do not judge, and you will not be judged. Do not condemn, and you will not be condemned. Forgive, and you will be forgiven.

Matthew **6:14-16**
For if you forgive men when they sin against you, your heavenly Father will also forgive you. But if you do not forgive men their sins, your Father will not forgive your sins.

When someone wrongs us we naturally feel resentment for that person. Scripture tells us repeatedly to forgive those persons. And I might add, we must forgive ourselves.

And not only should we look at forgiveness in a biblical sense, we should look at it at a more general, cerebrally healthy perspective. People who are generally more neurotic, angry and hostile in life are less likely to forgive another person even after a long time had passed.

We must keep in mind also that forgiveness is not to give the person who is being forgiven a pass on what they have done. It is to cleanse the soul of the victim so that he or she may be at peace.

People who are neurotic, angry or hostile tend to want to be forgiven for being the way they are. Yet they are not forgiving. What often results if they are not forgiving or forgiven is the overwhelming feelings of betrayal. This often results in despair, anxiety and depression. When this occurs, it can take a physical effect on the body. Perhaps the blood pressure would rise, or the heart will begin to race. Then they become more neurotic, angry and hostile.

Biblically speaking, persons who are not forgiving will have to deal with God at his time of judgment. Jesus speaks of this through a parable In the book of Matthews.

Matthew 18:21-27 (NIV)
Then Peter came to Jesus and asked, "Lord, how many times shall I forgive my brother when he sins against me? Up to seven times?" Jesus answered, "I tell you, not seven times, but seventy-seven times. "Therefore, the kingdom of heaven is like a king who wanted to settle accounts with his servants. As he began the settlement, a man who owed him ten thousand talents was brought to him. Since he was not able to pay, the master ordered that he and his wife and his children and all that he had be sold to repay the debt. "The servant fell on his knees before him. 'Be patient with me,' he begged, 'and I will pay back everything.' The servant's master took pity on him, canceled the debt and let him go."

Matthew 18:28-35 (NIV)

But when that servant went out, he found one of his fellow-servants who owed him a hundred denarii. He grabbed him and began to choke him. 'Pay back what you owe me!' he demanded. His fellow-servant fell to his knees and begged him, 'Be patient with me, and I will pay you back.' But he refused. Instead, he went off and had the man thrown into prison until he could pay the debt. When the other servants saw what had happened, they were greatly distressed and went and told their master everything that had happened. Then the master called the servant in. 'You wicked servant,' he said, 'I canceled all that debt of yours because you begged me to. Shouldn't you have had mercy on your fellow-servant just as I had on you?' In anger his master turned him over to the jailers to be tortured, until he should pay back all he owed. This is how my heavenly Father will treat each of you unless you forgive your brother from your heart."

Notice that Jesus said in the last line of the preceding scripture that you must forgive from the heart. This is very, very important. It is not enough to say "I forgive you", then every time you see that person your heart palpitates and your blood boils. You feel an uneasiness in the perpetrators presence. You must let go from the heart. Meaning that your forgiveness must be thorough and complete. This may be a difficult thing for anyone to do. Especially if the person has violated a trust so deeply or was so vehement when they were hurting you. However it must be done in order to allow yourself to heal and be at peace. The way to get there is through prayer. Pray for the person who has hurt you. Pray that God gives you the perseverance and strength to forgive. As well you must pray for that person, that God forgives him and causes him to see the error of his ways. Ask God for the perpetrators ability to forgive. Paul says, in scripture, that we must not hurt our bretheren.

Ephesians 4:31-32
You must put away every kind of bitterness, anger, wrath, quarreling, and evil, slanderous talk. 32. Instead, be kind to one another, compassionate, forgiving one another, just as God in Christ also forgave you

So. if your feelings are hurt and you have already started to pray for yourself and the one who has hurt you, what do you do now. Scripture says you not publically bring that person to task. That person must be made aware that he or she has hurt you. Scripture says you are to inform the person of the trespass quietly... one on one. So don't go broadcast the hurt and who hurt you on some social media page. Don't talk about it with a third party trying to gain sympathy or a supporter. These actions only breeds contempt for many people. It breeds contempt for you for stooping so low as to publicizing your private information. Publishing or making known the events that have occurred, breeds contempt from the perpetrator from the perpetrator's family and supporters. And it breeds contempt from Christians in general if you claim to be a Christian. If you are a Christian, let's handle this in a Christian way. And remember, that publishing your situation only perpetuates the longevity of the hurt and pain. Your aim should be to leave your past in your past.

Many times when we are hurt by another, we fail to look at our part in the situation. Sit down and meditate on the situation. Play the events back in your intellectual recorder (your mind) and evaluate what you see. Could you have done something differently? Could you have said "maybe" instead of "no". Could you have reacted differently? Could you have walked away rather than allowed a bad situation get worse? Were you out of control? Were you in control? In your mind, you may have had little to do with the result, however, in many cases the victims are not always one hundred percent victims and perpetrators are not always one hundred percent perpetrators. If you find anything you did to offend that person, you must apologize to him or her and ask for forgiveness. Be specific. Let the person know what it is you are apologizing for. Then leave it at that. Do not add any 'buts' or 'howevers' or 'if you didn'ts'... Your intention should be at this time to walk away or to hang up the telephone. But if they say something, you listen. More than likely they will tell you that they accept your apology. It is likely that they would apologize for their part. But if they do not, do not get angry all over again. Know that they have not reached the point of maturity that you have reached. Therefore their maturity is something else you must pray for.

Romans 12: 17-21
Do not repay anyone evil for evil; consider what is good before all people. 18 If possible, so far as it depends on you, live peaceably with all people. 19 Do not avenge yourselves, dear friends, but give place to God's wrath, for it is written, "Vengeance is mine, I will repay," says the Lord. 20 Rather, if your enemy is hungry, feed him; if he is thirsty, give him a drink; for in doing this you will be heaping burning coals on his head. 21 Do not be overcome by evil, but overcome evil with good.

Paul wrote, "Do not repay anyone evil for evil". This is pretty much self explanatory. In today's "gang" world, scripture is forgotten about. We hear on the news all the time of retaliatory murders. I have often asked myself, "How did we get this way?" The answer I come up with is how, in what manner, were these young men and women were brought up or raised. I remember, on the streets of Harlem, two boys were talking trash to one another. It was obvious that they were working up to a physical altercation. When the boys squared off to fight, one of the boys' mother was in the audience. She shouted, "You better kick his a.. or I will kick yours when you get home!" Not only was she condoning the fighting but she was perpetuating it by encouraging a fight. And if her son had lost the fight, she would have inflicted more violence on him. I have seen this same scenario time and time again throughout the United States. There is no diplomacy. There is no love in those words the mother shouted. She portrayed a parent who believed that her son should repay evil with evil and what is even worse; she is sending that same message to all her children and the other children that were out there to watch the fight.

Her children will likely join a gang mainly because of what they wrongly believe in. And believe it or not by the time the child has joined the gang, the mother usually recants her belief of repaying evil with evil. However, it is too late now. The damage to her children has already been done. And then there is the situation when the younger child follows the older child's footsteps, and so on. The next thing you know, we are attending double and triple funerals.

And then there are countries and governments who bear the same mentality. Some shoot and bomb other countries because their boarders were illegally crossed. Or they take over countries because their naval bases are threatened. Or they shoot their own countrymen because they threw stones at the army.

This type of indifference for life trickles down to the citizens of the world. It is no wonder that the mother is shouting to her son to "kick is a.."!

We live in a worldly society that does not seem to get it. Evil for evil only leads to more evil. Once you let the devil get a stronghold on your spirit it is only God that can get it back. However, it is our duty to allow God into our hearts.

What I am saying and what scripture says many times is that if someone has trespassed against you, you have got to let it go. Forgiveness is the answer. Let God and the laws of the land take care of it. You will be happier for it. You will be at peace. And this gives you time to do other things besides fighting.

Chapter Three

Honesty and What it brings

In different versions of the bible the words honesty, integrity and righteousness are interchangeable. Where honesty is used in the New International Version, the words integrity or righteous may be used in the English Standard Version or the King James Version. Honesty should not be interchanged with these words because honesty is actually a vehicle for one to obtain integrity and/or righteousness. Integrity and righteousness should be considered goals.

The simple definition of honesty is: The quality of being fair and truthful.

The definition of integrity is: the quality of being honest and having strong moral principles; moral uprightness.

The definition of righteousness is: the quality of being morally right or justifiable.

Both integrity and righteousness are the result of honesty. To have integrity generally means you are respected because you will generally do the right thing when called upon and when not called upon to do it. It means that even though your children will go with you kicking and screaming, to a dental visit, eventually they will realize that you are doing the right thing. It means that you will not fold under pressure when your peers are calling you to do something other than what you know is the right thing. It means that even though she is a pretty interesting woman, you will not go to bed with her, not only because she is married to another man, but because God has commanded you not to do so.

Righteousness is God given. Being righteous is a title that God gives believers before they are claimed as justified. In a nutshell, you must be justified to go to heaven. A way to become justified is to declare that Jesus died on the cross for our sins. However, there is more. You must also be righteous in the sense that you must have the quality of being morally right. In order to become morally right, you must have integrity. And to have integrity, you must be an honest man.

The bible gives us many verses on honesty. Here are a few samples.

Proverbs 11:3 (NLT)
Honesty guides good people; dishonesty destroys treacherous people.

1 Chronicles 29:17 (NIV)
I know, my God, that you test the heart and are pleased with integrity. All these things I have given willingly and with honest intent. And now I have seen with joy how willingly your people who are here have given to you.

Proverbs 12:22
Lying lips [are] abomination to the LORD: but they that deal truly [are] his delight

Proverbs 19:1
Better [is] the poor that walketh in his integrity, than [he that is] perverse in his lips, and is a fool.

1 Peter 3:10
For he that will love life, and see good days, let him refrain his tongue from evil, and his lips that they speak no guile:

Exodus 20:16
Thou shalt not bear false witness against thy neighbour.

Romans 12:17
Recompense to no man evil for evil. Provide things honest in the sight of all men.

There are some people who ascribe to the idea that says a Christian must be honest with everything. There are some women and some men that agree that in their relationships they should be totally honest. I do not agree that there ever has been a totally honest person on earth with the exception of Jesus himself. I do not believe that it is possible for a person to be totally honest. I also believe that it is not healthy to be totally honest. Total honesty leads to brutal honesty. And being brutally honest can lead to chaos.

In fact, at times we are totally dishonest. For example; we can have the burdens of the time on our shoulders. We could have the IRS, the Boss, the Pastor, the Wife and the children criticizing every aspect of our lives. We could have been diagnosed with cancer, tuberculosis, and diabetes all within one week of each other. We could be depressed and oppressed. Yet when someone asks, "How are you." It is instinctive to lie. We say, "Fine".

Being totally dishonest goes all the way to Adam and Eve when Eve asked Adam, "Does this fig leaf make me look fat?" A totally honest Adam would have said, "You're seventy-five years old, Eve. And you have put on 40 pounds since God created you. Nothing you put on can make you look any thinner!" This is an example of being totally and brutally honest. How do you think this verbal exchange would have gone over in your relationship today?

And then there is the Santa Clause thing. How would your three year old child react when you tell them there is no such thing as Santa Clause. And all of his or her friends celebrate the coming of Santa Clause and your kid is the only one insisting that Santa is his parents. He may find himself with no friends and scarred for live. He may even grow up to be a sociopath!

I am sure you understand by now that being totally honest totally does not work. However scripture says that Christians are to be honest in dealings with other Christians as well as others. At the risk of appearing to split hairs, I will go out on the limb and say that there is nothing in the bible that says we are to be totally honest.

Some people look at the subject of honesty in this way. People should be honest if it does not hurt others or themselves. I am suspect with those persons' cognitive thinking. What if you stepped out of your Christianity and you decide to partake in an indiscrete passion with a woman other than your wife. Your wife gets a text message from your new partner. When you get home you are confronted by your hurt wife. Do you think that admitting your despicable act will hurt her? Do you think that your admission would hurt you? Most would answer yes to these questions. You are looking at a situation that would hurt both you and your wife if you were to be honest. So you deny, deny, deny until you cannot deny any longer. Of course, you should have never practiced the indiscretion of being with another women, however it may be best for you and the family to start the healing process of your broken relationship as soon as you possibly can. When confronted would probably be the best time.

Or what if you took a pencil from your work station and placed it in your shirt pocket. You then inadvertently bring it home. You know that others have been fired for taking paper clips home. Your boss confronts you about the theft the next morning. You have a choice. You either admit it. And proceed to explain to your boss that you happened to place the pencil in your shirt pocket and forgot to take it out before you clocked out. You also tell him that you forgot to pick up the pencil from your dresser that morning but you will bring it back the following day. Or do you just say, "I don't know what happened to the pencil! I didn't take it!" Many people take the latter approach, not because they are bad people, but they would rather deny ever taking the pencil rather than have to give the boss a lengthy explanation. Believe me, there are many people who are willing to argue that they did not take the pencil all the way up to looking at the hard drive recording taken from the surveillance cameras.

There is a saying that goes something like this. "Never do something you will have to lie about later. If you have to lie about it, you shouldn't be doing it." Doing something you will not have to lie about later is an act that may be very difficult for some new Christians if you are or were like me at one time in my life, a big fat liar. I was drugging, drinking and cavorting and stealing as much as I could get away with. Not doing the wrong things was quite a challenge. I can't remember the amount of times I told a policeman, "I only had two beers officer". Or I looked my wife or girlfriend in the eye and told them, "I was hanging out with my friends" (Until three in the morning).

Lying and misleading people became such a habit, that some certain people never believed me anymore. And what's more, I would tell other people about how I lied to the policeman or to my wife. Now do you think that the people I told those stories to will ever believe a word I say again? So I became a person with near zero credibility. Not only that, but in the eyes of God, I was not righteous. I am no longer at that point in my life, thank you Jesus. But it took some work... Some mental work... and some God work.

Let's go back to that example about Adam and Eve when Eve asked if she looks fat in what she was wearing. Some psychologist would actually say that we (men) should ignore the question and give an answer to another question. We should say something like this. "That fig leaf looks fine, but you know, the red fig leaf looks so much better on you." If you have ever tried this approach you would know that you were actually being brutally honest and she will let you know. What she heard was, "Yes, that fig leaf makes you look fat. Now go change your clothes!"

The bible says we should encourage others. Eve is looking for some encouragement, right? So what is more important? To encourage her or to be brutally honest. Encourage her, for God's sake! It won't hurt you to say, "No, the fig leaf only makes you perfect!" Well maybe that's a little over the top, but you get the picture.

Ministers and church members do this all the time. No matter how well I do or how bad I do in giving a sermon, people are always telling me how the sermon touched them in some sort of way. That there was something I said that touched their hearts. I have never heard anyone say, "That was good, but if I were you, I would have said..." or they dare not say to me, "That was an awful message." We must be cognizant as to what we are saying to people if we want to do God's will and encourage them.

I remember when I dropped out of high school in the eleventh grade. I was the baby of the family and all of my siblings had already graduated. One had already attended college. It was the "end of the world" to my mother. She gathered all four of my older sisters and brother and told them the news. My oldest sister, said to me these words. "You are a smart and intelligent boy and I know you will go on to get your GED. You are probably too smart for school... Go on, do what you gotta do." These words, I will always remember. And I reminded her of these words about a year before she died. I went on to get my GED. I obtained an associates degree in business and an associates in legal administration. I went on to obtain a Juris Doctorate Degree. And, all of these silly diplomas I obtained while keeping my sister's words of encouragement in the back of my mind.

So, I guess what I am saying is, when you can choose from either honesty or encouragement, you should always choose encouragement.

Now let us look at the Santa Clause incident, when you told your three year old there is no such thing as Santa Clause because you decided that you wanted to be honest. I remember when I learned that there was no such thing as Santa Clause at the age of seven. It was devastating. A Jewish friend of mine told me, but I didn't quite believe it. I ran home and confronted my mothers and my sister. They decided that it was time to let me know the truth. They explained that mommy was the one who bought all the gifts. But they also told me that Santa Clause was in my heart. Whatever that meant! I went to school and told others, and about half had already known.

Now imagine, if you will, informing a three year old that there is no such thing as Santa Clause. When she is in preschool, around the holidays, she will be surrounded by other students who believe. And the teacher will have him or her make drawings of Santa Clause. Other kids will be talking about sitting on Santa's lap at the mall. There will be Christmas programs at the school depicting large jolly men in red suits at the end. Don't you think this child will be confused? Congratulations! You have just succeeded in making your child an outsider.

I say it again. Total honesty just doesn't work!

Now, let's look at the pencil disappearing from your cubicle. At work, I must say that 99.9 percent of the time, honesty works in your favor, unless, of course, your wife works with you and she asks you if she looks fat in her dress.

I worked for twenty plus years in a very sensitive position where mistakes were made all the time. I had trainees whom I would tell, "When you make a mistake, own up to it". "Never attempt to cover it up." "Let someone know, and perhaps they can help you make the necessary corrections."

The truth is that everyone makes mistakes. And believe it or not, mistakes are made to be forgiven. If you accidentally put a pencil in your shirt pocket, took it home and you get fired for it, then that job was probably not for you. Be glad! You don't want to be around unforgiving people who disciplines you for taking a pencil home. It only stresses you out.

So when should you be honest? Always, when you know being dishonest will interfere with your salvation. Tell the truth whenever possible. Think of it this way. Would God want me to be dishonest at this time? In order to get to this point you must remember to keep God in your mind and in your heart at all times. As a Christian, this is your responsibility. Remember that being brutally honest is evil.

1 Peter 3:10 says: *For he that will love life, and see good days, let him refrain his tongue from evil, and his lips that they speak no guile.*

Be compassionate and you will have good days.

Integrity and righteousness are what you are working towards, right? Integrity is a human word that indicates that you are a man of your word and of good standing. You tell the truth and you will do what you say you will do. That you have compassion for your fellow man. That you love only one wife or girlfriend. You do not get angry over little things. As a matter of fact you rarely or never show anger.

This seems like a tall order for some. But remember, Christianity is a process. The longer you stay true to the word of God and the more you practice it, the easier it gets. And the surer you are of your own righteousness and justification.

There are some people in the church as well as outside the church who will put you down because of a rumor they heard. They get things twisted and start repeating lies that either they made up or truths that are misinterpreted in their minds. These people do not normally deal in truth and honesty on its face value, but are usually looking for an angle to twist and maneuver the truth into something deviant. Remember, that their salvation is not your job. You do not criticize. You do not judge. Leave that for God. You may want to set the record straight, by telling the truth. You may want to walk away to give yourself some quiet time. Whatever you do, do it calmly. God is watching the way you react. If you are not being righteous, He will let you know.

People are watching you too. Cussing someone out because of something they said to you or to others about you is suspect of your Christianity. And so goes your integrity.

You see, once you cross over into Christianity, one of things you develop is something you may not have had before. It is called a conscience. Your consciousness becomes more keen to others sensitivities. Allow your conscience to take over your mind by allowing God to consume you. If you are aware that your conscience is a gift from God, then your day to day quests will be much easier. Be aware, at all times, of God's presence. Also be aware of the devil's influences. The devil does not have the power to make you do anything. But the devil will put suggestions in your head to knock that lady out or cuss her out, or to start spreading rumors about her. This is where your conscience should come in to play.

If you were to do something foolish and then had to repent or apologize for it later, then you did not allow your conscience to take over your mind when the incident occurred. You knew that you were doing something foolish, but you allowed the devil's influences to take over your mind and you managed to push your godly conscience to the rear.

During our day to day living, there are always going to be people who are less godly and less honest than we. And they will try to challenge us. We have to be prepared for them. We cannot control whatever it is that they do or say. We can only control our own actions and reactions (individually). God can be in control, but only if you let him. And if you let God consume you (as much as you possibly can) then you will see increases in your own self-control. However if you place your godly conscience to the back of your mind, then that action leaves a void to allow the devil's influences to enter.

Some people have been acting negatively all of their lives so that denial and aggression has become a way of reacting to life's situations. They finally get tired of the chaos and dysfunction that negativity naturally brings to them. So, when they come to Christ for answers it is extremely difficult for them because they have been questioning all things for an entire lifetime. And normally they give themselves the answers rather than seeking answers from others or from God. And since they are in a negative mindset, their answers are usually all wrong. To these people we ask, "How'd that work for you?" Oh yea, now you want to change your life.

Now they have a book (the bible) that claims to give them all the answers. They pick up the King James Version and don't understand most of it. The book is talking in a language they are not familiar with. The messages are sometimes rather subtle, and they don't get it. The preacher says to read the bible... to memorize versus. So they start selecting versus that they have some understanding of and start memorizing them. So, now they can quote scripture, but they know not how to apply it because they do not understand the context in which the scripture was written.

Be honest with yourself. Realize that you do not understand what you have read. Now go out and find the answers so that you do understand. Your pastor is probably a very busy man, so you cannot always rely on him being available to have all the answers you seek. Since the inception of the internet bible commentary has matured and expanded one hundred fold. Go to a search engine and type in the verse(s) you are researching, then type in the word commentary. A whole bunch of sites will appear to give you information on that verse.

Ask someone who is knowledgeable of the bible. There are people who have already gone through what you are going through as a new Christian. Most of the time, they will be willing to help.

I was once teaching a bible class and a question came up in the book of Leviticus. I did not know the answer. I went to two, older, seasoned, pastors and explained the question. One of the pastors actually said, "Well, you know, Uh, I haven't been studying like I should. I-I really don't know the answer."

I truly believe, God put me in his life, at that particular place and time, to make him conscience that he should be studying scripture again rather than to keep quoting the scripture that he memorized many, many years ago. The other pastor said, straight out, I don't know the answer." I believe God put me in his life at that particular place and time to wake him up! I don't think he even understood the question.

I later called my previous pastor. He gave me the answer off of the top of his head. He gave me explanations and examples. I was forever grateful. That pastor is now my 'go to' guy whenever I have a question. And I bug him a lot.

What I am saying is, find your 'go to' guy.

Get another version of the bible besides the King James Version or whatever version you have. My two favorite bibles are the King James Version and the New International Version. What I don't understand in one, I may understand better in the other. I had a pastor that told me that the King James Version was the only bible I should have. Sometimes the King James Version is a little too cryptic for me, especially the Old Testament.

Take your previous negative attitude and turn it to positivity by doing positive work. Do not allow negative Christians or others to get in the way of your positive work. Be both honest and positive in your quest for understanding. Honest and positive work yields honest and positive results. Do not pretend to understand.

There are some things all people must be honest about. That is they must be honest about themselves including their own attitudes and personalities. And there are many people who are very willing to let you know how they really think about you.

There is a saying that goes something like this.

If someone calls you a horses behind, you may want to ignore it.

If a second person calls you a horses behind, you may want to look behind you to see if you are growing a tail.

But, if a third person calls you a horses behind, you might as well strap on a saddle.

If you are a bully, stop bullying! If you are a liar, stop lying! If you are a thief, stop thieving! If you are scandalous, stop scandalizing! You do not need God or scripture to know these things are wrong. But you may need God to recognize them in you. If he sends three persons to tell you that you are whatever you are, then you can almost rest assure that He is trying get you to recognize that you have a problem. Some people have to get out of the mindset that what they do does not affect anybody or better yet, it does not affect themselves. Whenever you do something dishonest you are hurting yourself and others. The following is a poem that was written by Mr. Eli Hamilton which best illustrates what dishonesty brings. Mr. Hamilton was incarcerated for a dishonest trade when he started writing poetry.

Every time you tell a lie

Something inside you die
Something you can't see
*Something called ho*nesty

This poem is short enough to memorize and powerful enough to stop you in your tracks. How true it is that a lie will slowly kill off your honesty? Unfortunately, telling effective lies successfully inspires us to tell more lies. And the more lies one tells, the more their honesty wanes. Without honesty, there is no integrity and no righteousness. With no righteousness there is no sanctification. Without sanctification we are condemned to hell.

Sometimes we determine that survival is easier to maintain than honesty. That is, our babies may be hungry and we choose to lie to the welfare department rather than go to work at a fast food diner.

If you are poor, you may want to do something dishonest in order to make your poverty more palatable. Whether it be lying on a welfare application, or robbing a bank or borrowing money that you cannot possibly pay back when you promised. You must remember, that being poor is not a sin. However, what you do to lift yourself out of an unfortunate situation, such as poverty, may be. Being poor is only a temporary condition, so long as you endure it and seek the way out of poverty using God's influences, not your own conniving ways. The bible defines what you are going through as longsuffering. Keep in mind that longsuffering is not suffering for a long time. It is the patient endurance you must sustain while you are going through whatever it is you are going through. Rest assure that
God sees and feels your pain. And he will deliver you. He will also remind you during that deliverance that he is God.

However, if you are to take things into your own hands and do something dishonest, you are not allowing God to deliver you. As a matter of fact, he may not want anything to do with you at that time. He will leave you. The Holy Spirit that is in you will lay dormant. Then, if you go this route of dishonest self-help enough times, you will become convinced that you do not need a God to guide you.

1 Samuel 2:8
He raises up the poor out of the dust. He lifts up the needy from the dunghill, To make them sit with princes, and inherit the throne of glory. For the pillars of the earth are Yahweh's. He has set the world on them.

If God is the one who raises us out of poverty, as illustrated in 1 Samuel 2:8, then it is God who will make a way for us while we are in what seems to be desperate times. What I am saying is, there is no need to be dishonest to get yourself out of survival mode. God will allow you to survive while you are working on an honest way of getting yourself out of that situation, so long as you allow God to be in your life.

If you do not allow God to be in your life, then survival mode can become a way of life for a much longer period of time and possibly as long as you are here on earth.

However, there are times when survival mode does click in when you need it most and being dishonest may pay off. For example; I had a friend, when I was growing up, who was a petty drug dealer on the streets of New York during the early seventies. He was sitting in his girlfriend's house when he got a telephone call from one of his friends who dealt drugs using the same distributor. The friend told him that he had just gotten robbed by two guys at gunpoint of all of his drugs. A group of "the boys" then assembled at the drug distributor's house so they can figure out what to do. They decided they were going to search the streets and find these two guys and get their drugs back. The distributor gave the boy who got robbed a 45 caliber handgun to take with him. He placed it in his waistband in the small of his back. Then about seven of the guys went out looking for the robbers. They found the two coming out of a bar on Amsterdam Avenue and they ran up on them. My friend and the friend that was robbed was in front of the crew. The other five were close behind. The exchange went something like this:

"Hey!"

"What do you want?"

"You're the guys who robbed me!"

After quickly assessing the situation, one of the robbers pulled out a twenty-two handgun.

"So what!"

Silence.

My friend said he was nudging the other guy to pull out his forty-five.

"Pull it out!" "Pull it out!" he said to the other guy under his breath. But the other guy was frozen.

My friend said he looked back, and saw the five behind him were backing up. He instantly went into survivor mode.

"Go ahead pull the trigger, I'll pull this forty-five out and kill you both!" He motioned back to the small of his back and grabbed his waistband, all the time bluffing. "Go ahead, I dare you!"

The two robbers looked at each other, after they glanced at their little .22 caliber gun, then backed up and then took off running. A couple of years later, the one with the .22 gun was found beaten to death on a corner a few blocks away from where this altercation took place.

I am not too sure that God or the devil had set up this confrontation. I do know that the devil's influence as well as God's influence was involved in major ways. The devil had influenced all seven of those kids to be involved in the evil trade of drug selling. And the devil had also influenced the robbers to pick up the gun and to rob that kid. It was God who intervened and did not allow the friend with the forty-five to pull out the gun. For, if the .45 was pulled out, there is no telling how many souls would have gone to hell that night. Even further, God gave my friend the ability to think on his feet, by faking like he also had a gun that was bigger than their gun, so that the robbers would not shoot first. I firmly believe that without God, shots would have been blaring, blood would have been spilled on the sidewalks, and families would have grieved because lives would have been taken that night.

Was it being dishonest when my friend bluffed that he had a forty-five handgun in his waistband? Yes, indeed it was. But, maybe it was God telling him to do this because He did not want Satan to win this fight. My friend went on to join the Air Force and eventually receive a graduate degree. And, he was appointed pastor of a church in California.

If you find that you have been dishonest in an ungodly way, allow your conscience to take over. Now it would be time for repentance. Go to God in prayer. Tell him what you did. Tell him that you are sorry for what you did. Go to the person you were dishonest to. Tell them what you did. Tell them you are sorry for what you did. Now comes the hard part. Never do that dishonest thing again! You will find yourself being forgiven by God and most likely you will be forgiven by the person you were dishonest to. Yea, they may say something like, "I will forgive you, but I won't forget." Let it go! You have done your part. If you're true to your repentance, eventually your friend will see your heart as does God.

In conclusion, Keep God in your mind and in your heart at all times. Allow your conscience to take over your body before you do a dishonest act or lie. Doing this makes dishonesty quite difficult. We are to be honest when it is necessary to build integrity, which is all of the time. Assess your situation before answering any question or confronting a person for doing you wrong. Do not put yourself in a situation which you would have to lie at a later time. If you are dishonest for any particular thing, ask God for forgiveness and ask the person you were being dishonest to for forgiveness.

Chapter Four

Love

Love is many things to many people. We generally use the word to describe a feeling of great affection for something or someone. For example we love our children. We love to drive. Or, we love sweets. However, the Greeks were able to categorize the word love. They divide the word love into four different concepts. They are Storge, eros, phileo and Agape.

Storge is an affectionate love. The type of love one might have been born into. For example, a love for a child, or a love for a mother.

Eros is the passionate or sexual love. The word eros is the root for the English word erotic.

Phileo love is a brotherly love one would have for a close friend.

And agape love, is the unconditional love. It is the love that is described that God has for us. It is also the type of love we are to have for God and other humans.

God's love has and always will be that of agape love. Some would say, while going through some rough times, that

God's love is not available for them. However, the truth is that God's love is always present. Let me show you proof.

A little earlier in this book I had mentioned the crucifixion of Jesus. Let us say for argument's sake that we (you and me) are part of the crowd that watched him being crucified. I am attempting to make this more personal.

When Jesus came riding into Jerusalem on a donkey, he was greeted with cheers. They laid palm leaves in his path so that the ride into the city would be more gentle. Then Jesus went into the courtyard where they were selling the goods. Jesus was outraged and he turned over the vendors' tables. Then he was arrested.

The people who were for him at the time of his entry into Jerusalem were now changing their collective mind about who Jesus was. Does this sound familiar? Do you sometimes change your mind about Jesus and God's power? Do you have a problem with prayer when you are jobless? Do you curse the existence of God when someone close to you dies? Do you think twice when you read in the newspaper that a pastor is arrested? The truth is you change your mind about God and Jesus just as fast or faster than the people of Jerusalem. It should be easier now for you to place yourself in the crowd that allowed Jesus to be crucified.

I do not believe for a minute that everyone in the crowd except the Marys and Peter were for Jesus' crucifixion like many pastors and movies would lead you to believe. But, think about this. If you were one of the few in the crowd that believed that Jesus was indeed the Messiah, would you speak up? Would you be the one that shouts to "Let him live"? Perhaps this explains Peter's denial of Jesus. But that is a different story. The bible also says that there were some women present, Jesus' mother included, who were in much agony to see Jesus go through his pain. The truth is, if you, as a Jesus supporter, spoke up against the actions of an angry crowd, you may have been on the fourth cross on Calvary on that Friday.

Now imagine this. You are God. Yes, these final moments were prophesized by various members of the Old Testament. And you (as God) know exactly what is going to happen. So, you watch your son get arrested. You watch your son tried. You watch your child being beaten. You see your son being paraded through the streets of Jerusalem. You see people spitting on him. You see someone force a crown of thorns on his head. You see Roman soldiers nail your son's bloody hands and feet to the cross. You watch Jesus' bloody body being hoisted on the cross. You watch a soldier pierce Jesus' side with a sword.

Now, as one in the crowd, what would you have done? Would you have broken through the crowd and thrown yourself on Jesus' body to protect Him? Reflect upon the love you have for your son or your daughter for a moment. It is likely that to be of an unconditional agape love.

If you were God, would you have destroyed all of the people at Calvary at that moment? Probably. As God, you have that power.

After all the torture, after all the pain, after all the blood, after all the humiliation, Jesus still commanded for God to forgive them (both the believers and non-believers that were in the crowd).

And God did just that. He forgave us. He did not destroy the persecutors or the spectators. He allowed us to live. He gave us the opportunity to repent for our sins. Is that LOVE or what!

Keep this in mind each time you question the existence of God...each time you question his love... each time you commit an intentional sin. He loves us unconditionally. He forgives adulterers as well as murderers. He forgives thieves as well as liars. So long as we ask him. And he does it with unconditional agape love.

Now get this! Christians are to love one another and all others with agape love.

Luke 6:28
Bless those who curse you, pray for them which despitefully use you

That's right! Unconditional agape love is what you have to have in your heart at all times. That means that even though you were unexpectedly put on child support you still have to greet your baby's momma with a hug or at least with a cordial greeting. And the guy who threatened to beat your butt at work? You should shake his hand the next time you see him. Wow, that seems like a tall order! But that is what agape love is all about. It is loving God, your friends, your family, as well as your enemies, unconditionally. It means that you do not hold grudges. You do not seethe with hatred. You do not strike back. You do not blaspheme. You do not denigrate. You do not spit on and you do not cuss out. What you do is forgive!

Now for most people who cross that Christianity line, they ask questions about this type of love. "You mean to tell me the bible says I gotta love everybody, no matter what? How do I do that?"

I often remind others that Christianity is a process. Most people do not get baptized and suddenly "get it." What we have to do is practice love. And the way to practice love is to do this. **Always keep God on your mind and in your heart.**

The way to achieve keeping God in your mind and in your heart is simple. First you have to make a conscience decision to keep God on your mind. Whenever you walk down the street, whenever you get into a sticky situation, whenever you discipline your children or are being disciplined, think of Him. Whenever you are not thinking of God, catch yourself and think of his magnificence. Think of his grace and mercy.

Look out your window and observe his creations. Look at the trees and the flowers and the grass and the seas and the mountains. Imagine the power it took to create these things natural things. Look at the clouds and the sun, the moon and the stars. Think of him by forming a mental picture of God in the celestial heavens. Or think of his name. GOD! JEHOVAH! YAHWEH! Whenever situations come up think of Him, however you want to think of Him. Think of His power! Think of His mercy! Think of His Grace! Think of His Promises!

If you follow this exercise, you will be conditioning your mind to be more aware of His presence.

Keeping God in your heart will require a little more self control. Your heart has to do with your emotions and we know some people have more trouble keeping their emotions under control than others.

A pastor once told a class that the heart and the mind are actually the same. A question came to my mind that I did not ask at the time. I did not want to embarrass the pastor and I did not want the class members, who hung on to his every word, to embarrass me. I thought of Matthew 22:37. Matthew 22:37 is a quote from Jesus. It says in the King James Version, *"THOU SHALT LOVE THE LORD THY GOD WITH ALL THY HEART, AND WITH ALL THY SOUL, AND WITH ALL THY MIND."* These words are capitalized in my version of the bible because of their importance. Jesus proclaims this to be the first and great commandment. The reason I questioned the pastors statement was this. Why would Jesus make such an important proclamation to be redundant? If heart and mind are all the same, Jesus would not be saying the same thing twice in the same sentence.

I believe that the pastor, whom was a male, in this instance took a self-disciplined, masculine point of view. We, as men, tend to do this unconsciously. And when we do this we fail to bring in a woman's point of view. We do know that women are the ones, basically, who are known to be emotional. *Let me be gentle with this please Lord!* Women are regularly demanding that men become more emotional and men are regularly demanding that ladies get their emotions under control. Emotions are what come from the heart. Anger, jealousy, sadness, rage, laughter, beliefs, joy, and love are all emotions that come from the heart. Men (especially disciplined men) tend to look at emotions as something that need to be controlled. Women, on the other hand believe that emotions are needed to remain healthy or in some cases, alive. Men seem to believe that when emotions get in the way of living your life, it must be controlled. Women believe the same thing, only their limitations are less restrictive than that of men.

Therefore, men seem to think that all persons should have strong limits on over their emotions. Some men believe this more strongly than others. Hence the Pastor's point of view that the heart (which is actually synonymous with emotions) and the mind (which is actually synonymous with intellect) are the same. One can control the mind. Therefore, one should be able to control the heart.

How about this? Not having control of your emotions may put yourself in danger of losing your health, your job or your relationships have to be controlled. Most people call this stress. It is not an easy task to control your heart, however, the negative emotions that are festering in your body must be abated. You will have to use your mind to get the anger, jealousy, rage, unrealistic expectations, being unforgiving and resentments out of your heart.

Keep in mind that you are doing this to be able to have real agape love. And you cannot have what God is demanding of you if you still harbor these negative emotions.

While you have these negative emotions inside you the Devil is actively working to bring these emotions to the surface and in many cases it takes very little for you to be acting "out of character", as many people say. The Devil does not want you to act Godly. He does not want you to become more like Jesus. Remember, the Devil is building his own Army, and if you successfully make it to sanctification, you are one less person that will join him in Hell. Satan is always going to be whispering in your ear...trying to bring out that jealousy, or that rage. He softly says things like, "The only way she will understand you is for you to be mean!" Or, "The only reason for her to be out so late is that she has a man on the side!" Or he will tell you at a tense moment, "Roll up your sleeves and ball up your fist. There's going to be a fight!"

So, how do you get rid of these negative emotions? First and foremost, you have to recognize that you have them. Some of us have been building up defense mechanisms in our heart all of our lives. We overreact to situations and we see things that are not there. Or we over exaggerate whatever stress is there. We become verbally or physically abusive. But what we do not see is that these defense mechanisms have made us emotional wrecks. We have to recognize that we have a problem with what we thought was the solution (our defense mechanisms). Seek counseling. It could be spiritual, psychiatric or therapeutic counseling. However, spirituality is very, very important and must be a part of your rehabilitation.

I once had a good friend. I will call her Rose. She was five foot two and weighed all of ninety-five pounds. The problem with Rose is that she could not keep her mouth shut. If she felt her feelings were stepped on she immediately voiced her opinion. She ended up leaving her family (husband and three children) to live on her own. She lost her job because of two incidents where she was unable to contain her tongue and found herself being supported by her estranged husband. All the while, she was constantly arguing with her three children and husband about how she was being mistreated.

Rose was super intelligent. She was able to complete New York Times crossword puzzles. She was able to get along with many people from many different cultures because she took the time to read about them and hang out with them. She was excellent in math. She had a great sense of humor. But once she got angry, she was unable to control her tongue. She said some pretty hateful things to her children and to her husband; to the point that neither one of them really wanted to have anything to do with her.

One of her children had gotten married and she was not invited to the wedding. She had a granddaughter that was more than a year old that she had never met because her daughter chose not to introduce them.

Anyway, Rose slipped into a depression. Rose and I were in communication at the time. I had known from previous conversations that Rose did not believe in God. I nevertheless attempted to console her with scripture and tell her about God's Grace and Mercy without sounding like I was "preaching" to her. I and also her family had encouraged her to seek counseling or therapy. I was elated when she texted me to tell me that she was waiting for a call from her therapist to set up an appointment.

I am not sure what happened at the therapist office. Apparently, the sessions had brought some repressed memories to light because the next time I saw Rose, she was blaming her situation on herself. She said that she understood that she was the one that had brought on the separation of herself from her family. That if it were not for her big mouth, that she would still be working. She said that the hurtful things she said to her kids led to her not being invited to the wedding and to her not seeing her granddaughter.

I insisted that the relationship between her and her family was repairable. However, she did not see that it was. She emphatically suggested that there was no way out! I asked her to pray. Of course, her response was "You know I don't believe in that stuff!"

I often pray that Rose asked God for forgiveness just before she slit her wrist and her throat two days after our last conversation. Her teenage son found her bloody body on her bed.

The reason I tell this story is to impress upon you the importance of God's love. Yes it is important that we come to the realization of our shortcomings. However there are some of us who are not ready to handle the truth. When we come to that realization we have to also know that God is a loving God who loves us no matter what we have done in the past. If you feel that no one else loves you for what you have done in the past, know this: That God loves you and he is waiting to forgive you no matter what! All you have to do is ask.

I often wonder what would have been Rose's outcome if she had God in her life. What she would have done when she found herself in her predicament and she prayed instead of trying to fix herself, by herself? What would have happened if she did not go to a therapist? What would have happened if she had repented the days before she killed herself? What would have happened if she realized that God is and always will be all powerful? That He can make a way out of no way. That He loves us always without equivocation or conditions or fallacy. That He has so much power, that if you let Him love you, you will feel the warmth of that love throughout your body. That He can renew your mind.

Oh, what a wonderful God He is!

There are some of us that have love in our hearts but for some reason or another we find it difficult to say "I love you" to someone. Let's take a brief look at that. There are some families that do not express love or affection in ways that others do. For example, they do not hug. They do not fondle. And they do not caress. A family of this nature tends to spawn children who act the same way. Many times, the children are over achievers. However, just as many times the children look for love in other places that result in gang activity and early pregnancies. These children often are attracted to pimps and child molesters who train themselves in showing affection and love. They (the children) become self-loathing. Not to mention the drugs and alcohol that they take to numb themselves of what is missing from their lives. We, the children of dysfunctional families, have to remember to love ourselves first.

When children take these unnecessary paths in their lives, the parents tend to blame themselves, and many times this is done justifiably. Parents should reflect upon the mistreatment they have thrusted upon their children and make the necessary corrections in their own lives.

I have often suggested to people who loathe themselves to look in a mirror at least once a day to tell their reflection, "I love you". Another thing I tell them is to tell a different person each day that they love them. I also tell them to tell God that they love Him on a daily basis.

What this does is condition the mind to be more giving of love.

We must also learn to become great recipients of love. I know someone whose name is Rita. Rita is the oldest of eight children. Her parents were alcoholics and drug addicts. Her brothers and sisters were constantly fighting for space and recognition. The parents were able to pretty much keep the family together in spite of their addiction problems. However, in doing so, the children always witnessed the parents plotting and manipulating the welfare system, neighbors and other family members. Each one of the children became either drug addicted and or criminals. Rita became addicted to drugs and went to jail for attempted murder. Upon her release from jail she became "rehabilitated". Rita, however, was quite skeptical of the motives of others. She had witnessed so much manipulation all of her life that she was unable to trust the good intentions of others. When she finally got married her husband would bring her flowers. Rita's first response would not be that of surprise and appreciation. What she would do is ask her husband in a sullen voice, "What did you do?" Her husband was actually trying to show her affection by lifting her spirits and letting Rita know that he was thinking of her. He was trying to show nothing but the love he had for his wife. However, Rita thought that the flowers were a way of manipulating her. He was crushed. Yet he still kept on bringing her flowers on a fairly regular basis. About the third or fourth time he brought home some flowers and she responded in the usual way, he confronted her about her attitude. She went on to explain to him the environment she was raised in and he understood. He explained how he felt when she responded to the gift of flowers and she understood. This story ended with a happy ending, however you can see that not being a good recipient of love can lead to misunderstandings, arguments and tension.

Not being a good recipient of love can also lead to rivalries being extended longer than it needs to be. Let's say you are in a feud with someone. And you decide to be the bigger person. So you approach that person to offer an olive branch, in peace. That person does not want any part of your offering. So you walk away, knowing that you have done your best to restore peace between the two of you. However, now you have something else to be angry about. That person was not a recipient of the love you offered, and because of that you now have another resentment towards that person. And until that person decides to forgive you and ask God to forgive them, the feud will resume (at least in his mind).

Open your heart to God's love. If you can do this you can open your heart to the love of others. And when you do this you can love more freely. The best place to start this process is with prayer. The next step will be to work on your family. Do you have a mother or father you have been feuding with? Do you have a brother or sister you have not spoken to in years? Now is the time for you to contact them without asking them for a favor. Tell them that you want to reconcile. If they talk crazy to you, that is okay. You do not have to respond negatively. Just endure them for a while. Let them see you smile. Let them feel the joy in your heart. Let them see that you are painless. Apologize for anything that you may have done to them in the past. In some cases there may be too many things that were said or done to remember what got the feud started or perpetuated. Here a blanket apology may suffice. Just say that you are sorry for whatever your part was in this fight. Get it off your chest. This will definitely help you to go on with your walk in Christianity. You will free your mind of the negative and allow yourself the freedom to honor and love God the way he wants to be loved.

Next, go to your ex girlfriends and baby mommas and ex-wives, to apologize to them for being the jerk you know you were when you had broken up. If you were not a jerk, you can apologize for your part of the break-up.

All the while during this process you will be concentrating on keeping God in your mind and in your heart.

Now comes the tough part. Take an inventory of yourself. What is the argument that keeps on popping up between you and your significant other? Is the subject of the argument something that you repetitively do or fail to do? Look at that! Study it! Let God reveal it to you through prayer. Tell your wife that you will change, and do it. Tell her you are sorry. Tell her that you love her.

Now, there are your children who has to be addressed. Maybe apologies are not in order for your children, however there may have to be some correction as to the way they are being raised. Ask God to allow you to be a wise and consistent father. Show your children God (as you understand Him) and ask them to grow with you in Jesus Christ.

After these exercises, you will be ready to receive love and be free to express love and kindness to others. What you have done is emptied all of the resentments and hatred out of your heart by recognizing and apologizing for the wrongs you have done. Now you are ready to fill your heart up with the love you will be receiving from others. And you will be able to more freely express love to others without the regrets and sorrows getting in the way because the regrets and sorrows will no longer be there.

Agape love is not obtainable by all persons. And if it is, some persons usually are not able to express agape love to all persons. For these persons there is Phileo.

Philia refers to brotherly love and is most often exhibited in a close friendship. Best friends will display this generous and affectionate love for each other as each seeks to make the other happy. The Scriptural account of David and Jonathan is an excellent illustration of *phileo* love:

1 Samuel 18:1-3
After David had finished talking with Saul, Jonathan became one in spirit with David, and he loved him as himself. . . . And Jonathan made a covenant with David because he loved him as himself

However, we are to have this type of love for all persons. We cannot just pick and choose who we cannot love and who we can. And we must always attempt to obtain agape (unconditional) love for all humans.

THE KINGSMAN

Chapter Five
Forgiveness

Ephesians 1:7
In him we have redemption through his blood, the forgiveness of sins, in accordance with the riches of God's grace

Isaiah 43:25
I, even I, am he that blotteth out thy transgressions for mine own sake, and will not remember thy sins

Luke 13:34
Then Jesus said, Father forgive them for they know not what they do...

Matthew 6:14-15
If you forgive those who sin against you, your heavenly Father will forgive you. But if you refuse to forgive others, your Father will not forgive your sins.

First of all we must understand that forgiveness is a process that actually cleanses those that are forgiven as well as those who forgive.

Forgiveness cleanses the ones who are forgiven because they are reminded that whatever negative actions they take can affect others and to not do them (the negative actions) again. Forgiveness of the person who has sinned against another allows him or her, who may feel they are facing retribution or revenge, to rest easy. They no longer have to be looking over their shoulder for the car screeching around the corner, or the frying pan being hurled at their head, or the knife between their shoulder blades. They can rest assured that the person they victimized will not hurt them. That is, if they are truly forgiven.

The forgiving person is cleansed because they are relieved of the anger which often follow being wronged or sinned against. They no longer have to plot revenge. As well, they no longer have to be angry about what was been done to them. They no longer have to be seething with the pain that was caused by the act of another.

It has been said that God forgives us for anything and everything. No matter what we do. No matter what you say that offends him or offends any other man or woman... He will forgive you. You can beat your brother senseless... You can lie about your friends... You can steal from your mother. You can even curse the name of The Father... God will forgive you. All you have to do is ask.

Isaiah 43:25

I, even I, am he that blotteth out thy transgressions for mine own sake, and will not remember thy sins

God is telling these words to Isaiah. This scripture actually says that He blots out our transgressions. Blotteth out is a biblical term for blot out or forget. A transgression is a violation of the law. And we know that at the time of the writing of this scripture, the violation of the law (as it was given by God) was a sin. So therefore what this scripture is telling us is that God has the ability to forget our sins. Isn't that a great thing?

It is said in scripture that if we sin, we die. It may not be that we die on this earth but what it is really is that we die spiritually. Isn't it a great thing to know that God does not want for us to remain spiritually dead. Isn't it a great thing to know that God's grace and mercy will lift us out of the darkness and into the light. Isn't it great to know that God has the power to lift us out of spiritual death. It's because of His ability to forgive. And not only that, He forgets! Isn't it good to know that he forgives! Isn't it good to know that he forgets. Isn't it good to know that he blots out. Isn't it good to know that he gives us grace and mercy. It is good to know these things about God's character because for many of us, if God did not forget, blot out and give us His grace and mercy, we would be not only spiritually dead but physically dead as well, and celebrating anniversaries in the depths of hell.

Have you ever done something you wish you could forget? Have you ever done something you wish you could just blot out of your mind? Have you ever done something that was so shameful that you have never told anyone about it? Well God saw you while you were doing it. And you know what? If you have asked him to he has forgiven you. And what's more, he has forgotten about it?

We as humans, don't have the ability to forget, unless we are afflicted with some unfortunate disease or head injury. If someone tells you they are sorry for something they have done

THE KINGSMAN

or said to you, You tell them, "I will forgive, but I will not forget!" Or, you tell them "Forgiven, but not Forgotten!" Well guess what. Who cares!? You don't have the ability to forget it anyway. "Forgiven, but not forgotten". That's just another way of saying, "If you do it again I'm gonna have to beat you down", or "I am going to have to get revenge"!

Maybe over time the memory will fade. Maybe you'll get into an accident and have an injury that afflicts your memory... But, generally, you do not have the ability to forget, anyway. And nowhere in the bible are we instructed to forgive and forget.

So what do we do if we cannot forgive and forget. We forgive with our eyes wide open. And to do that we should be spiritually driven. If someone asks for forgiveness and then asks a favor of you, you should oblige them. You should love them as you do yourself. You should love them as you do Jesus. But don't fall for the okey doke! The okey doke was something Mohammed Ali had invented. Later, ring announcers called it the "rope-a-dope". When he was fighting George Foreman, Mohammed Ali would pretend to be hurt. He would be covering up and lean on the ropes while pretending to be hurt. George Forman would be wailing away at Ali. Keep in mind that Foreman had a right cross that could stop a bus. Ali would be covering up...leaning on the ropes... walking around the ring. And when Ali sensed that George Foreman was tired, Ali came back at Foreman and literally beat him down. Ali knocked Frazier out with an uppercut.

Don't be like George Forman, who by the way became a great two-time champion. Don't fall for the okey doke. Keep your eyes open and use your energy wisely.

Some of us are not spiritually driven. We are not recognizing the okey doke because we are not listening to the

84

spirit. Open your ears as you open your mind. Open your eyes as you open your heart! Allow God to speak to you at all times.

Many of us feel we've been kicked around all of our lives and we remember the trauma we felt like it was just yesterday. In some instances it was yesterday!

So what is our job, as Christians, when it comes to forgiving someone.

Matthew 6: 14-15
For if ye forgive men their trespasses, your heavenly Father will also forgive you. But ye not forgive men their trespasses, neither will your Father forgive your trespasses.

Matthew 6: 14-15 is a promise made by Jesus. Now I ask you. Has God ever gone back on his promise? Has He ever not brought you up or brought you out of the messes you have gotten yourself into? If you have asked him, has He ever not forgiven you? Even when you have deliberately gone against his word, he has forgiven you.

Scripture says the penalty for sin is death! And I am still here! After all the trespassing I have done. All the drugs I have done! After all the partying I have done! After all the drinking and carousing I have done. After all the lying and stealing and cheating. I am still here. He promised me. He promised me that all I have to do is forgive. And he would forgive me.

It is a difficult thing to do; to Forgive.

Literally, to forgive means to stop feeling anger toward (someone who has done something wrong) : to stop blaming (someone).

Some of us have been let down so egregiously that we can't find it in our hearts to forgive. The lies, the deceit we have been subjected to... The beat downs we have suffered... The torment we have gone through... Sometimes we find ourselves being no more than a shell of a person. We suffer humiliation at the hands of another! And when the other person comes to us to ask for forgiveness we normally reply, "I forgive you." But do you really? Do you still harbor the anger? Do you still blame that person for the shame you felt?

If that person came to you in need, would you help them? Would you open your pocketbook for that person? Would you open your heart for that person?

I was talking to a person about this subject. He said to me that generally he is willing to forgive people for doing him harm. However, there is one person that treated him so badly that he will not help him if he came to him for help. I told him that his heart has been hardened, like Pharaoh. You know the scripture in the book of Exodus, when after the people of Israel left for the promised land. Pharaoh's heart was hardened and he and his army took off after the people of Israel to recapture them. And I am sure you know the end of Pharaoh's story... He was swallowed up by the sea.

Are you being swallowed up by the sea? Are you drowning in hate? Are you plotting revenge? Are you wallowing in rage? Are you asking to be forgiven but are not willing to forgive?

When it comes to forgiveness, God has two things he can do that we cannot do. One thing which we have already discussed. That is, God has the ability to forget. The other is that He has the ability to look into our hearts. Now most of us think we are good judges of character. We think that we can look at a person and judge whether they are a good person or not. But, the truth is, sometimes we are mistaken.

Have you ever been tricked? You would be looking a person dead in the eyes. He would tell you all the things you wanted to hear. Ladies, (if there are any women daring to read this book) you know what I'm talking about. He would sweep you off of your feet. He would tell you he would take care of you. He would be loving all over you. He'd buy little things for you to show you the affection he has for you. He'd promise to never leave your side. Somewhere along the line you have convinced yourself that you are a good judge in character. You would convince yourself that this is a good man. Then all of a sudden you find yourself in a relationship that you wish you could get out of. And every time he leaves or you manage to put him out, he comes back and apologizes. He asks for your forgiveness. And you let him back in. You thought you could look into that person's heart. Don't be deceived! We do not have the ability to look at a person's heart.

Or, to you men out there. Have you ever talked to a lady and they said something like, "I don't need a man to support me!" And they start waiving their head. They do that side to side neck thing that they do. Then they say something like, "I'm an independent woman!" So you start popping bottles, and buying them things because you see this lady has potential. She can take care of you while you take care of her. But then you find out that the real reason she doesn't need a man is because her babies are receiving welfare and she don't know who her babies' daddies are.

The point is, as much as we think we can judge a person's character, we cannot. Only God has the ability to look into a person's heart.

And why is this important? It's important because when you say to the one who offended you, "you are forgiven." God is looking in your heart. He is looking for sincerity. He is looking for gratitude. He is looking for sorrow. He is looking for humility. If you don't have it, you are not truly a forgiving person. And if you are not a forgiving person, you are a sinner. And, once again, if you sin, you die that spiritual death. As well, if you are asking to be forgiven, God is looking into your heart.

So what do we do? We say the offender is forgiven but we bring up the offense time and time again. We plot revenge. We remain angry. Christian people's minds are supposed to be at rest so that we can keep God on it! People's hearts are supposed to be clear of negative emotions so we can keep God in it! The holy spirit cannot possibly live among all that negativity that we spew from our lips or all of that garbage that is rolling around in our minds. Nor can it possibly dwell in all of that hatred in our hearts.

We must find a way of emptying, from our body the negative emotions and filthy thoughts so that we can make a room for the blessings of our father. One way is to not to be a thankless forgiven, and to be a fervent forgiver.

Now, what about being forgiven. When you ask to be forgiven, you have to recognize what it is you are being forgiven for. Not for the other persons sake, but for your own sake. To recognize your sin, means that you will sincerely work on not committing that sin again. Also be thankful for being forgiven.

We get into arguments with someone, and we know that we are right about what we are arguing about. We argue with anger. Has anyone ever not argued with anger? If you know you are right about the point you had to make, don't ask to be forgiven for arguing your point. Ask to be forgiven about the way you delivered your point. Was the yelling and screaming really necessary? Did you have to poke your finger in his or her face? Did you really have to slam that door? Did you have to stomp your feet? That is what you have to be forgiven for.

And when you ask the other person for forgiveness, ask God for it too. Because the holy spirit cannot dwell in an unclean house. You have to purge yourself of that anger and rage. Ask God for forgiveness so that the holy spirit can take over your heart and your mind. Since the Holy Spirit is a comforter, it will show you how to get rid of your anger or at least give you peace.

Some of us have done things, whether intentional or not, to hurt someone. Sometimes, we don't see the suffering they have gone through. We don't see the nights they cried. We don't see the sadness in their hearts. We don't see the pain they endure. But you know, somehow, God has a way of bringing the suffering of others to our attention. And it is at that very moment we must ask for forgiveness.

My God is a great God! My God is a merciful God! My God is a gracious God! He knows what I need. And I need to be forgiven.

You know how I know that? Because he gave the earthly life of his son for me. And when he did, he did the ultimate in forgiveness! You know why it was the ultimate act of forgiveness. It's because I didn't even ask for it!

He watched as his son was tried for heresy. He watched as his son was drug through the streets.
He watched as his son was forced to carry a cross through the streets. He watched as his son was spat on and beaten. He watched as his son was sweaty and bloodied. He watched as his son was humiliated.
He watched as his they laid a crown of thorns on his head. He watched as they tied his hands and nailed them to the cross. He watched as they tied his feet and nailed them to the cross. He watched as the people yelled Crucify Him! Crucify Him. He watched as they raised his son attached the cross on Calvary.

And he listened when his son said in Luke 13:34, "Father forgive them for they know not what they do". And we did nothing to stop the Romans from crucifying Him.

And then he did just that. He forgave us! He forgave us! He forgave us! And he forgave us time and time again. Since then, over and over, we have committed horrendous sins. Sins against humanity, sins against God's creations, sins against God himself. And over and over he has forgiven us. The proof of that is that we are still here; alive and kicking. If you weren't, I doubt if you would be reading this book!   We have been given the opportunity to redeem ourselves and sanctify ourselves to the likeness of our Lord and Savior, Jesus Christ, only by God's grace and mercy.

Now there is the issue of forgiving ourselves. Sometimes we punish ourselves through our thinking. We convince ourselves that we do not deserve to be better at life because of what we have done in the past. We beat up ourselves for things we have done in the past.

For example: Do you have a difficult time disciplining your children. Maybe, you are going easy on them because you think they deserve a better life you had in the past. Maybe you have been easy on them because of all the years you neglected them because of your unavailability. Maybe you were incarcerated or maybe you were on drugs or alcohol. So now you give them the run of the house. You allow them to smoke weed in the house, or you allow them to have seedy friends over to the home. Or when they talk back to you, you cry or pout instead of putting your foot down.

On the other hand, maybe you overreact to situations that are unimportant. Maybe you are always lashing out at family members or others.

Another example is that in the past you have done a lot of dumb stuff and when you finally decided to stop doing that dumb stuff, you were constantly hitting a brick wall. The dumb stuff you were doing before has been catching up to you (either physically or mentally). Very few people trust you. Some people don't even like you. You can't get ahead because you are always running into your past. Old traffic tickets, child support, a dirty drug test, etc. So, therefore your past becomes your present. The only difference is that you no longer do the dumb stuff. However, what happens is that you are now in a rut because somehow you start to believe that you do not deserve any better than what you have now. So you struggle to make amends with people. You try to pay off your old bills that you have neglected for years. You call your mother, your ex-wife and your children to ask them for their forgiveness. But you still have a feeling that something is still dirty about you. You have lived such a dumb life, mostly all of your life, so now you have come to believe it is time to suffer the consequences. You may have no contact with your children, you may have no food to eat, you may even be living on the street. But you think that that is okay, because you are only suffering because of the dumb things that you have done in the past.

Not true! The reason you are suffering is because you have not done the one thing that must be done after living a potentially disastrous lifestyle. You must forgive yourself! God has forgiven you and you must find a way to say, what you did in the past was not okay with God. And, at this time in your life, you must be able to say that your past is okay with you, your present is temporary and your future is going to be just fine. Now, at this time, when I no longer do dumb things, there are two things I must remember. The dumb things I used to do are part of my testimony. The second thing is, my successes and achievements after His forgiveness and intervention. Of course I am not going to say that you will always be successful. You will still do some dumb things that stifle your success. That is okay. Can you move on now? Can you stop wallowing in your own pity? This is what is important. So move on! Go on! Live on!

Or maybe, you are a pretty good guy. You attend church every Sunday. You go to bible study. You have taken on a position with an auxiliary. And you are gay. You hear all the time in church how men should not lay down with men nor a woman with a woman. You look around and you notice that women are coupled off with men. If you are 'in the closet', this starts to wear on your conscience. So now, you feel bad about being gay. You start to feel that being gay means you are not loved by God as much as he loves others. Not because it is true, but because you hear others confirming its truthfulness.

Forgiving yourself is about letting go of resentments. It is not about getting away with anything, such as being a closet gay person. Nor is it about attempting to forget that you have a certain sexual preference. Acting in these ways will only cause you more pain and confusion. The pain, anger and confusion you feel is not something you are supposed to feel. Feeling pain, anger and confusion while you are in church can only influence your determination to move away from the church.

Some people feel that it is only the scripture and God can help you to get over this anguish you feel. The truth is, sometimes religion leaves us confused. Interpretations of the bible vary not only from denomination to denomination, but from church to church and person to person.

If you are gay and feel uncomfortable in your church, go to another church. I say this, of course, in light of some denominations that insists that you should be converted to a straight heterosexual. But, in the meantime, you cannot serve

God comfortably and wholeheartedly if you are carrying a lot of excess baggage in your heart and on your mind. And you cannot begin the process of forgiving yourself if you are constantly reminded of how bad you are or how bad you used to be.

God has given us all many talents. Some have talent to counsel people on certain issues. If you are a drug addict or alcoholic you may have found yourself in a Narcotics of Alcoholics Anonymous meeting. However, at these group meetings you will find many people who are spiritually bankrupt. There is a lot of talent in those meetings to get you to stop using drugs. However there is little there to get you saved. I guess, what I am saying is that you may want to seek some outside intervention to assist you with certain problems. The Anonymous groups are certainly places to help you solve some of those issues of your past and the personality problems of your present. And even though the anonymous groups were actually founded on spirituality, do not expect to get saved there.

Look to religious leaders to assist you with coming closer to God. Look for some outside groups to seek the help you may need outside of spiritual assistance.

You may want to get some counseling from someone other than your friends or pastor. See if it helps. Pastors' and friends' intentions are well, however, some of us need more assistance than pastors who are afraid to tell you that they are inexperienced. Most church members' conception of the pastor is that he is "all knowing" and that he is "clean". And friends will generally tell you what you want to hear.

Are your kids always yelling at you or being defiant? Most of the time it is not entirely your kids fault. Are you and your spouse always arguing? Many times it is not entirely your spouses' or mate's fault when something goes wrong in the relationship or household. However, we argue, to show that we are right. Sometimes we argue to avoid issues. It could be your own reaction to your spouse's rational thinking that is contributing to the dissention, apprehension, and tension in the household. Counseling, especially good Christian based counseling could put you and your relationships back on track so you can stop being angry and resentful to yourself and to others.

Remember that it is important for you to free your own mind of torment before you can truly love God. If you have a lot of resentments and/or anger within your heart and mind and you try to love God, chances are you will end up using God as merely a tool for getting rid of the resentment and anger. As a result, if you are not relieved of these resentments or angers by a certain time, you will blame God for allowing it to go on. It is not God's fault you are not taking care of yourself. God has placed a lot of talented and experienced people on the earth for every individual's benefit. Take advantage of God's gifts to us. Make a good honest attempt to get rid of the anger and resentments that have festered for your lifetime. By doing this you will be able to forgive others and to be a grateful forgiven.

Chapter Six

Prayer

Prayer means many things to different people and there are just as many ways to pray. There is public prayer and there is private prayer. There are prayers for healing, prayers for protection, prayers for petition, prayers for thanksgiving and Prayers for worship. There are prayers on your knees, prayers standing, prayers with heads bowed, prayers with heads raised, prayers with arms raised with palms facing out, prayers with hands raised with hands facing in, prayers with hands clasped. There are prayers that are said aloud. There are prayers that are said in silence. There are prayers using anointed oil, there are prayers using incense, prayers using sacrificial animals. There is morning prayer, there is evening prayer, there is grace. Some people pray twice a day, some pray six times a day. Some pray all day. And there is fasting.

Everyone has their way of communicating with God. This communication is called prayer. Now notice the word communicate. Most people understand that to communicate means there must be a communicator and there must be a communicatee. In a conversation, we alternate roles as communicator and communicatee. And so is the same with prayer.

People have had a powerful urge to pray to some higher being since the beginning of time. They would pray to idols and to certain pagan gods, depending on what part of the world they were in and their belief. They would pray for good crops, they would pray to win wars and they would pray for fertility amongst other things. They would pray to the sun, they would pray to the moon, they would pray to statues and statuettes.

Many of us fall down to our knees at the end of a day and ask for the many things we think we need to sustain our lives. We ask for money, cars, good children, mates and the like. Sometimes we ask for things we don't really need. And sometimes we ask for the necessities in life. Some would say that we should only pray for things that are necessary. However, the truth is that what is necessary and what is relevant, only to the individual person doing the praying.

I remember an episode in my life when I had about two dollars in the bank. I had a bill that absolutely had to be paid within the next twenty four hours or my telephone was going to be cut off. Like many others, my telephone is my lifeline since I receive all of my business through telecommunications. I had no money for food. And the dirty clothes in my hamper reflected that I also had no money to buy detergent to wash my clothing. I had been working so hard not to get to this point in my life ever again, yet I found myself virtually penniless. I did not expect to receive a retirement check for another week. I fell to my knees with tears in my eyes. I told Him that I thought I did everything that I was supposed to do. I worshipped Him, I took out adds, I handed out business cards, I showed love for everyone, I had a forgiving heart. So you see, I was doing the work. During my prayer I do not believe that I asked God for money. But I do remember asking Him to bring me peace and to relieve me of my anxiety. Before I said Amen, the telephone rang. It was a client offering me a contract worth enough to pay my telephone bill, to buy detergent and food and to have a little left over to last me until I got paid.

When I fell to my knees, I had an expectation that God was going to relieve me of my anxiety and fear because I knew of all of the work I was putting into this situation. I knew that he would not fail me. I did not know, however, that it would be so quickly that He would show Himself.

Prayers are normally answered in God's time. Not ours.

Some may have called this coincidence, but I know this was God responding to my prayer. God had known, in advance that I was going to fall to my knees at that certain time, on that specific day. He had already sent his angels out to make the incident happen to give my client cause to call me at that specific time, on that specific day.

What had occurred on that day has given me strength in future matters when I am feeling distressed. This one incident, that I always mentally refer to when I am distressed, reminds me that God is in my corner. So now when times get hard, I don't stress. I don't stress because I know that God will make a way for me. That God has a way of providing for me no matter what the need is. Since then, I have been up against deadlines with no money in my pocket. I simply say that I know that God will take care of it. Yes, I may have to do a little work, but it is God who guides my steps and allows me to go in the correct directions to receive His blessings.

I was talking to a preacher friend of mine, he told me this testimony. He said he was driving in the rain through Flagstaff, Arizona in an old clunker with a non-operating gas-gauge. He got about twenty miles pass Flagstaff and ran out of

Gas. He looked in his wallet, all he had was about 10 dollars. He looked in the trunk of the car and there was no gas can nor was there a receptacle to put gas in. He then started walking but before he got out of his car he prayed. So he started his trek to the nearest gas station. It was cold, the wind was blowing and the roads were wet. While he was walking he prayed. He looked for a large bottle or container he could use to put gas into once he got to the gas station. About a mile down the road he happened to look into the bushes that lined the road. He saw something red. It was a five gallon gas can. He picked it up. It was full of liquid. He opened the can and placed his nose on the spout. You guessed it. It was gasoline. He was convinced at that time and forever after that God answers prayers.

These examples are prayers that were answered immediately and with tangible results, however sometimes answers are more subtle.

I have a friend who was praying for a promotion on his job. He applied for the different positions at his company about four times. Each time he would pray incessantly for the job to be given to him. He never received the promotion. In fact, he received a pink slip and was expected to leave his workplace in about two weeks. It would appear that God never answered his prayers. However a week before he was scheduled to leave his job, another company contacted him and offered him a job with better hours and more money. This is merely a way of God letting my friend know that his prayers were heard, but God had wanted him to be humbled enough to accept what God had in store for him.

God answers prayer in many different ways. Whether it by a telephone call, a gas can or a job offer. He hears all prayer to Him. But we must all remember that whatever He does, He does it by using his own plan and in his own time. This is not to say that all we have to do is sit back and do nothing. Going back to my examples, God had given me the wherewithal to build a client base, so that when I was in need, a client delivered the telephone call at the request of God. God had told the minister to walk west instead of east so that he would find that gas can. And God had told my friend to work hard at this job so that he can be recognized by someone outside of the workplace. God wants us to work but he wants for us to put Him first. The acknowledgement of Him, through prayer, is a way for us to do this.

Matthew 26:41
Watch and pray, that ye enter not into temptation, the spirit indeed is willing, but the flesh is weak.

This verse in Matthews indicates that you cannot rely solely on your flesh to receive your blessings, no matter how hard you try. The spirit will guide you, therefore you must work and listen to the spirit. The spirit that is within you is of God. God is all powerful. Therefore, the spirit within you is stronger than any other part of your body. With all the positions of prayer; sitting, standing, heads bowed, bodies prostrate, hands raised, hands clasped; it matters not. Your spirit is the most important thing. Do you come to pray with a humble heart? Or do you demand things of God? Are you aware that no matter what it is you ask for or when you ask for it, it is His will that will be done. And His will be done in His time. It is very important to remember that God is the Father and the provider. He is the only one that has control. He is the one with the plan.

Jeremiah 29:13

And ye shall seek me, and find me, when ye shall search for me with all your heart.

When you pray make sure that your prayers are not just to ask for something for yourself or your loved ones. Make sure God is all right with you. Ask for forgiveness. Know that you are not always right with God because you sin daily. You must be humble. Approach God with thanksgiving and humbleness, or as the scripture says, "with all your heart".

God does not say he needs for you to be an eloquent speaker in order to pray. According to Jesus, there is an order for prayer that he gives the disciples in his recitation of the Lords Prayer, which I shall talk about later in this chapter. Speak plainly, so that you understand what you are asking for. Do not use words that you do not know the true meaning of. Do not use words that you heard an elder use during a congregational prayer. Prayer must come from your heart, not someone else's.

Ecclesiastes 5:2
Be not rash with thy mouth, and let not thine heart be hasty to utter any thing before God: for God is in heaven, and thou upon earth: therefore let thy words be few.

Matthew 6:7
But when ye pray, use not vain repetitions, as the heathen do: for they think that they shall be heard for their much speaking.

Know what you are merely a human and you are speaking God who is all powerful. When you speak to him, there is no need to repeat the same thing over and over again. He heard you the first time. Chanting is frowned upon in most denominations. As well, there is no minimum nor is there a maximum amount of words for you to speak to God. But don't babble.

Matthew 6: 9-13
Our Father which art in heaven, Hallowed be thy name. 10. Thy Kingdom come. Thy will be done in earth, as it is in heaven. Give us this day our bread. And forgive us our debts, as we forgive our debtors. And lead us not into temptation, but deliver us from evil: For thine is the kingdom, and the power, and the glory, for ever. Amen.

In Matthew 6:9-13 Jesus teaches his disciples a prayer which is modernly broken down into sections that some theologians say should be followed when you pray. Personally, I attempt to take heed to the teachings of these scholars, however, there are times when it is not practical to think that we are to pray in the manner they teach. For example, it would not be practical to pray in a formal manner if you are merely thanking Jesus for allowing you to get through a tough time. Or when you have just won a game of Yatze. During this time you may want to say a simple prayer like, "thank you Jesus."

Anyway, the way that many theologians break the lord's prayer down is this. First we must acknowledge who we are talking to. "Our Father which art in heaven..." This is a distinction from any other father we may have. We call our dads father, we call priests fathers, we call step dads father, yet neither of them can be spoken of to be in heaven unless they have already passed on (and even this is controversial). So this is a distinct address to God. Further we say "...Hallowed be thine name". This is giving tribute to the being we are speaking to. As well it further distinguishes the being you are speaking to. Hallowed means holy or to recognize as being holy. What this says is, "Dad, Priest, Step-dad, who have already passed on, I am not speaking to you right now." "I am speaking to the Holy Father, God."

"Thy Kingdom come." Is informing the lord that you are ready to accept his kingdom and his word. For it is his kingdom that is what is the destination for all of His people. You are asking for His Kingdom to come to earth. As well, when you say "Thy will be done," you are letting God know that even though you are asking for the things you are asking for, you know that, in the end, it is His will that will be done. Not yours, not anyone else's.

"On Earth as it is in heaven," means that you are asking God to bring His control and His will to the world. You are also letting God know that you know that He has full control over heaven and earth. You are asking him to take full control over the earth.

We ask God for our necessities when we say, "Give us this day, our daily bread". Necessities may include housing, clothing, education, work.

We owe God a lot. He has given us life and he has given us opportunity yet we squander it by not listening to his word. Yet God is a forgiving God. So we ask him to "forgive us our debts". Some bibles say to forgive us our trespasses. And, I am sure that you now know how important it is for you to forgive. Therefore, you are reassuring God that you are forgiving the ones who trespass against you. This is represented in the passage that says "as we forgive our debtors or trespassers.

"And lead us not into temptation" is a little bit mind boggling. Would God ever lead us into temptation? I would think not. Perhaps this passage means that we shall never believe we are led into temptation by God. For if we were to ever think we were led into temptation by God we will not ever trust Him. "But deliver us from evil," is asking God to shield us from the evils of the world.

Towards the end of the prayer we once again acknowledge God for who he is. "For thine is the kingdom, and the power and the glory, forever. " You are acknowledging that you recognize that God has the ultimate power in His kingdom. You let him know that you know that God is all powerful. And you are letting him know that you know that he deserves the glory. Not only in the past, and not only in the present, but forever.

"Amen," simply means so be it.

So, you are thinking, this is what I have been saying all these years. But I still don't understand... Theologians say that when you pray 1. Make sure you address God as God Almighty. Acknowledge him and distinguish him from all other gods and from all other fathers; 2. Thank him for the blessings he has given you in the way of necessities; 3. Ask for forgiveness; 4. Ask him to keep an eye on you and to lead you not to go astray from His word. And end the prayer.

The Lords Prayer is one of the most simplest and most humbling prayers there is. It asks for nothing material, only what is promised from God. It does not ask to hit the lottery, or a fine lady to become a wife nor does it ask to make the children behave. All of these things are pretty much material. Material things are what we tend to ask for whenever we pray. Remember when you pray to thank Him for the blessings you have already received. Most of us have bread or food in our pantry, yet we ask for filet mignon. Most of us have a car or adequate transportation, yet we ask God for a top of the line Mercedes Benz. We have clothes to wear, yet we ask for designer labels. We must remember when we pray that we must be humble. Thank him for what he has already done for you. Remember that you have been delivered by God's grace and mercy and you would not exist if it were not for that fact.

As well, in demonstrating your humility, pray for others. Ask God to bless others who are less fortunate than you, especially. Pray for the homeless, pray for your crazy ex-girlfriends, pray for your drug addicted cousin, pray for the lying politicians as well as the neighborhood gang members. Pray for the people who have done you wrong and pray for the people who has done right by you. Whoever is on your mind (besides yourself) should be the focus of your prayers. If you are walking in the spirit, you will not have to pray too much for yourself. I believe God loves and rewards humility.

If you are going through a difficult time during your life and you find it hard to focus, pray for yourself. Ask God for forgiveness, but do not ask for blanket forgiveness. Be specific with the sins you know that you have committed. Ask him to restore your mind and/or your body to where it use to be or to strengthen your mind and body to where He wants it to be.

But in the meantime, you have to be accountable to your own stability. You have to do something. If eating right will correct the problem you have, eat right. If money will solve the problem, discover new ways to make money honestly. If wellness will solve your problem, go see a doctor. If mental illness is your problem, go see a psychiatrist. If you are walking in the Spirit, God will bless the food and the job, and the doctor, and the psychiatrist to be able to assist you. However, most of the time, just sitting around, dormant and waiting for your prayers to be answered probably will not make God very happy. I have found that he does not respond to prayer if you do not do the footwork.

Matthew 14:18

He said, bring them hither to me.

Jesus put the disciples to work after they told Him that there was not enough food to feed the crowd of people. Jesus did not suddenly make the five loaves of bread and two fish appear. He could have, but he did not make filet mignons and decanters of wine to feed the masses. What he did was, he had the disciples go fetch the fish and bread to bring them to Him. He put them to work. Then he blessed them with enough food to eat to feed the crowd.

Another example is the children of Israel when they were wandering through the wilderness. God had them walking with little food and little water during their quest for the promised land. They had to work to receive God's blessing. In spite of the promise God had made them to receive the promised land, they had worked hard to keep their psyche and physical health together. While they worked their faith was tested. They finally were blessed with God's promise, yet they had to work to receive the blessing. See the books of Matthew 14 and Exodus 14.

Psalm 62:5
⁵ My soul, wait thou only upon God; for my expectation is from him.

Pray with expectation. By now, you should know the power of faith. Let God know that you have an expectation of Him blessing you with whatever you ask for. Go forward as if there is no other alternative but to receive God's blessings in all of its glory. Know that God will answer your prayer. Your expectation is a reflection of your faith. Know that God heard your prayer.

When I fall to my knees, I have an expectation that God was going to relieve me of my anxiety and fear because I knew of all of the work I am putting into any situation is in his name. I know that he will not fail me. I do not know when he will show himself but I do know that he will.

Prayers are normally answered in God's time. Not ours.

Chapter Seven

The Fruits of the Spirit

When Jesus was preparing to leave this earth, he assured his disciples that God was going to send something to them. That something was a comforter. This comforter was to abide with us forever. This comforter was to teach us. And this comforter was to remind us of Jesus' teachings so that we can remember Him as He was, and is, and forever shall be. This comforter was the Holy Ghost, or as some were come to know it as the Holy Spirit.

John 14:16 and 26
16 And I will pray the Father, and he shall give you another Comforter, that he may abide with you forever;
26 But the Comforter, which is the Holy Ghost, whom the Father will send in my name, he shall teach you all things, and bring all things to your remembrance, whatsoever I have said unto you.

Now, I wanna say, that the Holy Spirit makes many people react to its presence in many, many different ways. As in the book of Acts, the remaining disciples were speaking languages they were never taught. To some, the holy spirit may cause you to speak in tongues. To some, the Holy Spirit may cause you to speak the good news wherever you may go. To some, it may make you fall to your knees to lift up his holy name, time and time again. And then to some it may cause tears to fall from your eyes uncontrollably. But all in all, the Holy Spirit is our comforter.

The Holy Spirit reminds us of the presence of God in each and every one of us. The Holy Spirit reminds us of everything Jesus has taught us. And in all of our trials; in all of our tribulations; in all of our sickness, in all of our bad situations, it comforts us by reminding us that there is a way out. That God provides us and shows us the way to a joyous heart.

Even during our temptations; and after the evil things we may have done. And after the evil we have been exposed to, the Holy Spirit remains our comforter.

Praise be to God. He is merciful!

Jesus gave up his life. And after doing so, God sent to us the Holy Spirit.

What is the Holy Spirit? It is an entity of God. Just as God had sent his entity, Jesus, to us to teach us a way of life, he also sent the Holy Spirit to remind us of the teachings. By doing so, God is telling us that He has influence over all of life and everything. The Holy Spirit is the vessel in which He uses today to remind us of that. The Holy Spirit can also discern good from evil and right from wrong, and it readily conveys this information to each individual. Let us explore this further.

Have you ever dated the "wrong person" for too long? Have you ever made a decision that you knew was right at the time but in the end you discovered that your decision was the wrong decision. The voice inside your head likely sent you a warning that what you were about to do was the wrong thing to do. For example; in the back of your mind, you knew this was the date of the Devil sent to you to destroy you. Or there was a nagging voice in your head that said that the people you were hanging out with were not of the best character, therefore they will surely drag you into something uncharacteristic of yourself. Instead of hearing this voice that you call your conscience, try labeling the voice as the Holy Spirit sending you a message that what you are encountering is not of God. Personally, I believe that our conscience and the Holy Spirit are intertwined. Sometimes we do not listen to our conscience. We should be more willing to listen to God through the Holy Spirit. You will find yourself making less mistakes in the long run.

By embracing the Holy Spirit, rather than ignoring it, you are placed on a path to righteousness. The more you learn to embrace the Holy Spirit, the easier discernment becomes. You will be able to separate the good from the bad and to become a better decision maker. Most people call this ability wisdom.

Paul Reminds us to "Walk in the Spirit" in Galations 5:16. Walking in the spirit is allowing the spirit to engulf you in its comfort. Let's say the spirit is a pair of new shoes. The shoes are uncomfortable. So you take them off every opportunity you get. You get home, you take them off. You get in the car, you take them off. You go to a friend's home, you take them off. You go to church, you take them off. And every time you wear them you stretch them out a little more. You find that you can wear them longer before taking them off again. Before you know it you are walking and sitting without thinking of removing them. They actually become comfortable.

Walking in the spirit is very similar. Wearing the Holy Spirit feels uncomfortable because it is something we are not familiar with. We are used to "walking in our stocking feet, or our old tennis shoes." We are used to doing things of a sinful nature. So every now and again, we have to take it (the Holy Spirit) off. We will remove the Holy Spirit, until the swelling goes down. Then we will place it back on our feet when we feel the time is right.

Has anyone removed the Holy Spirit sometime this morning, when you were getting the children ready for school? Has anyone taken off the Holy Spirit sometime this week when you spilled the raspberry Kool-aid on the beige carpet? Has anyone forgotten the Holy Spirit when something did not go quite right for you at your job this month? All of us have, all of us do take off the Holy Spirit, at one time or another, when it is not comfortable for us. And when we remove the Holy Spirit from us, we say and do things that Christians are not supposed to do or say.

However, Paul tells us to walk in the spirit. Yes, it may be uncomfortable for us, and yes it may even be tight on those corns and calluses. But if you keep on walking in the spirit, it will conform to you. It will become 'comfortable'. Some say you can throw a little polish or mink oil on it to help the process along. The polish or mink oil, in this case, would be prayer and worship. Pretty soon, those hectic days will not be so hectic. Those children will not be so bothersome. The job will go right for a change.

Another point I want to make is this. We are not to blame the Holy Spirit for anything bad or evil. The Holy Spirit is of God. And everything that is of God is good. So when we walk away from the Spirit, it is not the Spirit's fault that we stray. Keep in mind also, that even though you may stray away from the Spirit, you still remain of God (because he created you), therefore you are good also. And God will allow you to reclaim the Holy Spirit at any time. But do not stay away from the Holy Spirit for too long for your flesh may find it difficult to reclaim it.

The Spirit is full of God's messages and mercy. In spite of what you may think of the shoe analogy, the Holy Spirit has not, does not, and will not change. It just molds to you for you to use as God pleases. And is given to you for you to use as you please. God has his intention of how you should use it and people have their own intention of how they want to use it. You will have to make up your mind. Do you want to please people (including yourself) or do you want to please God. It is up to you to take advantage of what God has offered you.

Paul, in Galatians 5, defines the Spirit by what it isn't.

Galatians 5: 19-21
19 Now the works of the flesh are manifest, which are these; Adultery, fornication, uncleanness, lasciviousness,
20 Idolatry, witchcraft, hatred, variance, emulations, wrath, strife, seditions, heresies,
21 Envyings, murders, drunkenness, revellings, and such like: of the which I tell you before, as I have also told you in time past, that they which do such things shall not inherit the kingdom of God.

You may note that some things have been left out of this list. However, the phrase "… and such like" in verse 21, is an indication that Paul may have forgotten to specifically name some things that are not manifested by the spirit. However, it is clear that "… and such like" also covers unnamed actions such as greed, homosexuality, and thievery.

For those of you who are new to Christianity, "If it is not moral, it is not of God." And if it is moral by today's standard, but is listed under Galatians 5: 19-21, it too, is not of God. Therefore, neither of these are fruits of the Spirit.

So, now we know what the fruit of the spirit is not. What is the fruit of the spirit?

Galatians 5:22 and 23

22 But the fruit of the Spirit is love, joy, peace, longsuffering, gentleness, goodness, faith,

23 Meekness, temperance: against such there is no law.

Love is something we have spoken about in previous chapters. It is a deep affection for God and for one another. Love is something that is rarely mentioned in the Law (the first five books of the bible) but is something that has been mandated by Christ in the New Testament.

Joy is knowing that God is always in your corner no matter what situations, devastations or tragedies that may occur in your life. Joy is the feeling you have when you know that God has the ability and will make all situations better. To know this is to know the joy which transcends from the feeling. And sometimes, God takes his time doing things. Joy helps you to be rest assured that God already has an answer for your relief and he has already disbanded his angels to help you out of your aggravation.

Peace is what results when you have harmonious relationships. Peace is calmness. Peace is looking into the eyes of a long time enemy and the heart never flutters, the blood pressure never rises and the perspiration never formulates. Not only do you have good relationships with others, but what is more important, you discover a harmonious relationship with God.

In spite of the physical make-up of the word, Longsuffering is not suffering for a long time. Let us make this clear from the beginning. Longsuffering means patient endurance. Sometimes we go through things that are dramatic as well as tragic. We wait for it to be over. Sometimes we take matters in our own hands. The fruits of the spirit provides for us the patient endurance so that we are able to get through these trying times without blowing our brains out, or blowing out the brains of another.

Gentleness is the expression of humility and kindness. It is putting the needs of others before your own.

Goodness is the opposite of evil. Keep in mind that there is some credence to the saying "Good overcomes Evil". Being good is the act of being positive by nature. Goodness makes you, what you do and what you say, desirable to others.

Faith is the belief of something that has not yet materialized.

Hebrews 11:1
Now faith is the substance of things hoped for, the evidence of things not seen.

If you continue to attend church you will hear this scripture over and over again. It is a reminder that if you are hoping (praying) for something to occur or to materialize, this thing you are hoping for has not been seen except for in your imagination. Your faith is the trust you have in God that he will manifest this occurrence so that whatever you are hoping for will come to past. Faith is also the belief in Jesus and that his earthly death on the Cross was for the sins of us all. Once again, you did not see it, but faith allows you to believe that it was done. And faith is also that God is all powerful, he is merciful and gracious. You cannot actually see it but you know it.

Faith is something that we use in our every day walk in life. When we walk on a sidewalk without looking down at the pavement. Our faith lies in the one who did the finish in the sidewalk, that it is smooth enough and that the large blocks are not unevenly paved. You have the faith that your foot will not hit an uneven corner and trip you so that you go tumbling onto the unforgiving concrete. You also have faith in your mother, that she will provide for you and protect you and guide you as you are growing up. You also have faith in your spouse, that she will not cheat on you, or that she will wash your clothes. You have this faith because you have repeatedly walked on the sidewalk before, your mother nor your spouse has never failed you before and you are hoping that they, including the pavement worker, never fails you in the future. Your walk with Christ is similar. You must believe that he has never failed you before. Sure, there has been times when you have blamed God in the past for your shortcomings or some negative event that has happened to you in the past, but ask yourself at this point... Was that really God's fault? Remember that when Jesus spoke of God he spoke of Him being good. And it is His good that God intends for you.,

Mark 10:18

And Jesus said unto him, Why callest thou me good? there is none good but one, that is, God.

So therefore, since God is Good, you cannot possibly blame him for the bad things that have happened to you. Would you blame the concrete paver if you tripped on a tree root when you were not watching where you were walking? Would you blame your mother for being hungry when you were not at home? Would you blame your spouse when your favorite shirt did not get washed when you left it in the car? If any one of things ever occurred, you will still continue to have faith in your concrete paver, your mother and your spouse. And as such you should continue to have faith in God after something did not go quite the way you expected or wanted it to go.

Yet, the biggest point is that you have faith in what you have not seen. The unseen is God. You see the results of His creation every day. Just like you see the results of concrete pavers work, and you see the results of your mother's work (in the person you have become or want to become) and you see the results of your clean house provided by your spouse.

Take a look around you. Of course you see murders, you see child molesters, you see crooked politicians. But do you not see people helping one another? Do you not see the miracles of new medicines. Do you not see the sun rising every day? They are all good things, that are results of God's unchanging hand. You didn't see him do these things, yet he did. Who else has the power to do it?

Meekness is not weakness. Meekness means showing patience and humility. Being meek also means that there is an air of tranquility about you.

Temperance is self-control or self-restraint. The fruit of the spirit will not allow you to indulge in a sinful nature. It will not allow you to take advantage of others even if you would enhance your own way of life. The fruit of the spirit provides you with strength to overcome temptations and the wherewithal to know when temptation is in your midst.

The way Paul explains the fruit of the spirit is to say that the spirit is a live entity that bears fruit. It is up to us to take advantage of whatever fruit the spirit bears. Walk in it, taste it, eat it. If you stay in the path of the spirit, it will provide all that

Paul said it does. However, like most of us, we stray. We go on another path. And normally that path leads to misery. Straying from the spirit may give you temporary satisfaction, however, these paths are normally roads to self-indulgence, sexual immorality and maybe even drunkenness. Not to mention all the other things in between. Becoming astray subjects us to everything that is against the teachings of Christ. And then there is the conscious which you will have to deal with.

The Holy Spirit may cause you to do many things but most of all it will comfort you. By walking in the spirit it may cause some to speak in tongues. To some it may reveal your gifts of prophecy. Or to some it may reveal and or enhance your talents. And yet to others, it may just cause you to keep focused on God and the rewards that comes to you. But most of all it will comfort you. If it does not comfort you, chances are, it is not the Holy Spirit.

I have included the following verses for your study. You may have to read these scriptures it up to ten times before you realize the important correlation between the fruits of the spirit and your life of Christianity.

1 John 5:14King James Version (KJV)
[14] And this is the confidence that we have in him, that, if we ask any thing according to his will, he heareth us:

1 John 5:15King James Version (KJV)
[15] And if we know that he hear us, whatsoever we ask, we know that we have the petitions that we desired of him

James:1:2-4

[2] My brethren, count it all joy when ye fall into divers temptations;
[3] Knowing this, that the trying of your faith worketh patience.
[4] But let patience have her perfect work, that ye may be perfect and entire, wanting nothing.

Zephaniah:3:19
The Lord God is my strength and he will make my feet like hinds feet, and he will make me to walk upon high places. To the chief singer on my stringed instruments.

James:1:20
For the wrath of man worketh not the righteousness of God.

Psalm:145:8
The LORD is gracious, and full of compassion; slow to anger, and of great mercy .

Isaiah:40:31
But they that wait upon the LORD shall renew their strength; they shall mount up with wings as eagles; they shall run, and not be weary; and they shall walk, and not faint

Galatians 5:22
But the fruit of the Spirit is love, joy, peace, longsuffering, gentleness, goodness, faith,

Romans 14:17
For the kingdom of God is not meat and drink; but righteousness, and peace, and joy in the Holy Ghost

Nehemiah 8:10

Then he said unto them, Go your way, eat the fat, and drink the sweet, and send portions unto them for whom nothing is prepared: for this day is holy unto our Lord: neither be ye sorry; for the joy of the Lord is your strength.

Chapter Eight

PRESS TOWARDS THE MARK

We look around us. We look into the world. We look at our politicians. We look at our schools. We look at our children. We look at our neighbors. Some of us look at our spouses. Whether publicly or privately, we are so willing to criticize them of their evil and wicked ways. We see that they are missing the mark. We see mass killers in Boston , Fort Hood, New York, San Bernardino and we tell ourselves that there is no way the perpetrators will get to heaven. Yet we fail to fall short of looking at the person who should be the most important person (other than God) who we should be evaluating. Many times it is we ourselves who are not understanding our duty as Christians. Sometimes the person the three important fingers that point at ourselves are overlooked as the index finger is pointing elsewhere. Sometimes we are missing the mark. We are reminded by Paul that we are to keep pressing towards the mark. Yet we still criticize, we still create ill will, we still argue, we still have differences of opinions, and we still judge. We have to discover what it is that is important in our walk with God.

Philippians 3:1-14King James Version (KJV)

3 *Finally, my brethren, rejoice in the Lord. To write the same things to you, to me indeed is not grievous, but for you it is safe.*

² Beware of dogs, beware of evil workers, beware of the concision.

³ For we are the circumcision, which worship God in the spirit, and rejoice in Christ Jesus, and have no confidence in the flesh.

⁴ Though I might also have confidence in the flesh. If any other man thinketh that he hath whereof he might trust in the flesh, I more:

⁵ Circumcised the eighth day, of the stock of Israel, of the tribe of Benjamin, an Hebrew of the Hebrews; as touching the law, a Pharisee;

⁶ Concerning zeal, persecuting the church; touching the righteousness which is in the law, blameless.

⁷ But what things were gain to me, those I counted loss for Christ.

⁸ Yea doubtless, and I count all things but loss for the excellency of the knowledge of Christ Jesus my Lord: for whom I have suffered the loss of all things, and do count them but dung, that I may win Christ,

⁹ And be found in him, not having mine own righteousness, which is of the law, but that which is through the faith of Christ, the righteousness which is of God by faith:

¹⁰ That I may know him, and the power of his resurrection, and the fellowship of his sufferings, being made conformable unto his death;

¹¹ If by any means I might attain unto the resurrection of the dead.

12 Not as though I had already attained, either were already perfect: but I follow after, if that I may apprehend that for which also I am apprehended of Christ Jesus.

13 Brethren, I count not myself to have apprehended: but this one thing I do, forgetting those things which are behind, and reaching forth unto those things which are before,

14 I press toward the mark for the prize of the high calling of God in Christ Jesus.

Philippians 3:1-14 is the recounting of Paul's life by his own words. And he tells us that after he met Christ, on the road to Damascus, he decided that he wanted to be more like Jesus.

In Philippians 3:1 The scripture starts off with, "Finally my Bretheren". Paul must have been a preacher because as you can see Philippians 3:1 is in the middle of the book. Don't you love it when the preacher says the word "Finally" only to find out that he had 45 minutes to go. Commentators have said that the word finally does not mean that he has reached the end of his letter, it is the end of an idea. It means is that he is emphasizing the rule... to "Press Towards the Mark.

Anyway, in the opening of this chapter he encourages the Philippians by telling them to rejoice in the Lord. He lets them know he is not going to discipline them. His intention is only to educate them.

In verse two Paul tells them beware of dogs. Beware of evil workers, beware of concision. The word concision is Paul's way of calling Hebrew leaders mutilators of the flesh or persons who think that circumcision is the way to get closer to the Lord.

At the time Paul wrote this he and the Hebrew priests were at odds. The Hebrew Priests were calling anyone other than people of their religion, dogs and evil doers. Paul just turned the words of the priests on them.

Paul announced in verse three that Christians are the ones who worship God in the Spirit and rejoice in the name of Jesus Christ. In contrast, he was saying that the Hebrews were putting all their trust in their works and in their birthright.

They were constantly writing new laws. They were circumcising their young men. They were dressing well. They were driving new chariots. Living in large clean houses. Getting educations. And they proclaimed that they are good Jews because they had been able to accomplish these things. But Paul wanted to bring to their attention that these things mean nothing without a relationship with God.

He said, we should worship God in Spirit, Rejoice in Christ Jesus and have no confidence in the flesh, which was proven by the life he led. For if the flesh rules you, this means you are enslaved to it.

So here you are, you are dressing well, you are driving large new chariots, getting educated but you are not building a relationship with God. You are building a relationship with the world because you put such pride in what you have or what you have done, rather than pressing for the mark.

And what is the mark? Paul would say, the mark is to be with Jesus after we leave this place called earth. The mark is to wear the crown. The mark is to sit at the footstool of Jesus' thrown.

Instead, what we want is more. ...More material things. There has to be something more to life than more. We have money, but we want more. We have cars but we want more. We have a home, but we want more. We want more money, bigger cars and bigger homes. We want better jobs. We want expensive clothing. We want to be dripping with jewelry. More, more, more!

What Paul is saying is that he had it all when he lived as a Jew. He had more. He had a birthright as a Jew. He was educated. He spoke at least three different languages. He was of royal blood. And he gave all of it up. He gave it all up in exchange for something even more... For his chance at immortality... For his chance to sit at the footstool of the thrown of Jesus.

Now Paul, I am sure, is not asking the Hebrews and the Philippians to give up what material things that they had. What Paul is telling them, however, is what they have here on earth is not as important as what they will have in Heaven if they live this life correctly.

He is also telling us that, even if you are educated, like he was, do not look down on people just because they are not. Even if you are a wealthy person, like he was, do not look down on the homeless and deprived. If someone is not dressed as well as you, do not talk about them behind their back.

Before that day Paul met Christ on the road to Damascus, he ridiculed the church. He looked down on the followers of Christ. He followed the religion of Judaism and he merely mimicked the behavior of his forefathers.

But after he met Christ on that road he realized that all that he had was mere 'excrement' . The wealth, the education, the material things was (as stated in the King James Version) merely dung(v.8). He realized that the only way for him to live was to emulate Christ Jesus. He determined that his works, his achievements, his Gucci shoes, his white chariot with the gold trim and the 36 inch spinner rims were no longer important. He determined that what was important was to <u>Press on towards the Mark</u>

And make no mistake about it. Paul did not denounce his Judaism. He added to it. He enhanced his Jewish faith by accepting Jesus as the messiah who was prophesized in so many parts of the old testament.

In this passage Paul does not come out and say so, however he implies, that religion can be harmful to Christians. Christians have separated themselves by denominations and in so doing we have a tendency to identify with the differences between themselves and others rather than the similarities.

For example, I have an aunt whom I went to visit in New York. She is of different denomination than I. We were taking a bus from one end of Manhattan to the other. Keep in mind that the borough of Manhattan is approximately 13 miles long. Considering that our bus darts in and out of New York traffic, and the traffic lights on every corner, the ride takes about 45 minutes. During that ride all she could talk about was death. She was trying to persuade me that we do not die an earthly death, then go to Heaven. All we do is sleep until we are resurrected. And we are not resurrected until Armageddon.

I have another friend who wanted to debate bibles and was adamant when he told me that all we have to be is good people on earth, then we will assuredly go to heaven.

Another friend has told me, that we do not receive the Holy Spirit until we speak in tongues.

I have also heard from another friend that said people who speak in tongues are merely attention seekers.

I was listening to the radio today and a pastor said that the Sabbath was on Saturday. He even went on to say that if you have been educated you would know that the Sabbath is on Saturday. And if you know that the Sabbath is on Saturday and you still celebrate the Sabbath on Sunday, you are sinning. The problem I have with this logic is when God created heaven and earth and he rested on the seventh day, I don't believe a calendar was invented yet.

All of these people are Christians. They believe that Christ came here and died for our sins. However, they are missing the point. Even though these people spoke with the zeal and enthusiasm of any experienced Baptist minister, they are missing the mark. They are merely parroting what they heard and what they have come to believe. Are the minor differences between denominations really that important in the eyes of God? I think not.

Most religions believe in a monotheistic theology, with one God. I dare to say, their God is the same God that we believe in as Christians. There can only be one God.

The truth is that these attitudes of decisive division merely breaks up the Church and separates humans from each other. It makes us confused. Unfortunately, many people concentrate on differences between denominations rather than what we all have in common. These people are missing the mark! And what is the mark? It is to be more like Jesus so that we will be welcomed into His kingdom.

What is important is that we all are to strive to be more like Jesus so that we can be accepted into His kingdom, whenever, that may be.

In Christianity there are way more differences than similarities between denominations. However, all denominations have the one similarity. We should all be pressing towards the mark. We are all pressing for immortality. Being with Jesus is the ultimate goal.

James 1:25, 26 (KJV)

25 But whoso looketh into the perfect law of liberty, and continueth therein, he being not a forgetful hearer, but a doer of the work, this man shall be blessed in his deed.

26 If any man among you seem to be religious, and bridleth not his tongue, but deceiveth his own heart, this man's religion is vain.

James is saying, getting people to be your religion is not a priority. It is vanity. It is puffing up. Getting people to have a relationship with God is the priority. Getting people to believe what you believe in, is not.

However, religious people are always trying to get you to see things their way. James says to listen, not run your mouth! Work on your relationship with God. Press towards the mark.

Everyone has their own interpretation of how they are to press towards the mark. I assure you that one way is not to convince people that your way is the best way.

I have five steps of my own that should be taken. You can take them if you want. You may want to add to them. You may even want to skip one or two. There is no guarantee that this is the right way, however, it is what I believe, is working for me.

How do we press towards the mark?

First we have to surrender.

When we think of the word surrender, we think of giving up. We envision that we are embattled and weakened to the point where we are willing to place ourselves in the hands of the one or the thing we have been battling against for so long. We throw up our hands and a white flag and say, "I give up". "Do with me what you will". We think of prisons and slave encampments.

And in some ways this is true. But God is the only being you can surrender to and get the Victory at the same time. Instead of prison and slave encampments he will give you freedom. He will give you a clear mind. He will give you eternal life. I am so glad that I can surrender today to a being that is so magnificent, so glorious, so superb, so merciful, so mighty, so loving and so caring.

We are enslaved to so many worldly things. Even after we walk down the aisle to accept Jesus as our Lord and Savior, we remain enslaved to things. It was not too long ago, I was on Facebook when I saw an entry of church member, It is not my intention to out the member. I am not even going to say which church. Anyway, a member placed a picture of a brandy bottle and a brandy sniffer on her page. The caption said, "Now, it is time to relax."

I have walked up on people who just exited the sanctuary and were in the parking lot. They were using foul language. Generally they'd turn around to see me standing there and apologize right away.

I have heard of church members that were entrusted with the keys to the sanctuary, stealing all of the electrical instruments and amplifiers from the church.

I have also heard of church members promoting and selling tickets for a gospel concert that was not going to take place.

These are people who have not completely surrendered to Jesus yet. They may be getting up the courage to bring out the white flag. And I have no doubt, they will eventually. For none of us are without sin, however all of us have the opportunity to surrender completely. And all of us want more than just sin.

Surrendering is not just accepting Jesus as your Lord and Savior. But, it is an actual change of direction in the lifestyle. It is also an undeniable faith you have in Gods love for you.

The second thing we have to do to Press Towards the Mark is to Repent. This is a little different because it actually involves talking with God and listening, understanding and obeying His guidance.

You have to let God know that you are sorry for the wrong you have done. However, I am not one for blanket repentance. You know what I am talking about. "God, I am sorry for all the wrong I have done."... Be specific! You cannot possibly remember all of the bad things you have done in your lifetime all at once, however, while you are driving down the highway, you will remember something you had done to make someone feel bad, or hurt someone's reputation, or made a policeman put you in handcuffs. Ask the lord to forgive you. God wants to know that you are sorry for what you have done. So when that sin comes to mind, you had better address it to God.

In the bible, Jeremiah, Ezra, Ezekiel, Jonah, and other profits were all calling for the Hebrew nations to repent. They did it to save the nation. We need to repent to save ourselves.

We have to Press Towards the Mark!

Repentance is not just apologizing. It is having a change of heart. When you repent you know that what you are being sorry for has gotten in the way of Pressing Towards the Mark. And since Pressing Towards the Mark is the ultimate goal, you can never do whatever you are repenting for again.

Number three is to forgive others. Forgiving others may be the most difficult of the steps for Pressing Towards the Mark. Many of us have unforgiving hearts. The bible often refers to this as "Hardened Hearts".

Matthew 6: 14-15 :
For if ye forgive men their trespasses, your heavenly Father will also forgive you. But ye not forgive men their trespasses, neither will your Father forgive your trespasses.

Many of us have held grudges against others to the point that we have actually forgotten what the grudge was about. As well, many people stress over the grudges they hold against other persons, as well as the grudge that may be held against them.

You cannot possibly have God in your heart if you are stressing or unforgiving. The truth is that there is no room in your heart for God if you are not a forgiving person. The bible says that God will not dwell in an unclean temple. If your heart is cluttered with stress and unforgiveness then it may be unclean. And if it is unclean, there is no room for God to enter. He may not be there for you. You can ask for his forgiveness all you want, but he will not forgive you if you are not a forgiving person. Matthew 6: 14-15 says so.

You cannot possibly be Pressing Towards the Mark if you are not a forgiving person because God has not forgiven you.

The fourth thing to Press Toward the Mark is a dialogue with God. Talk to Him. Let him know what you want, but let him know that it is His will that shall be done. Let him talk back to you. Listen to Him.

Believe me, in spite of what anyone tells you, you do not have to learn how to pray. All you need is the Lord's Prayer, and some other words to come out of your mouth.

I remember attending a church in South Carolina. The pastor of the church asked a deacon to lead us in prayer. Boy, could he pray! He had the congregation shouting Amen and Hallelujah about ninety percent of his twenty minute prayer. I remember thinking, "I wish I could pray like that". Then it came to mind that God hears all prayer. Jesus said all you have to do is pray the prayer that he taught the disciples. A simple prayer... the prayer we have come to know as the Lord's Prayer. This tells me that all you have to do is talk to God. It matters not that you quote scriptures from the bible. It matters not that you are eloquent in your speaking. God knows what is in your heart, however he wants you to express it with your mouth. And in doing so, you will find God will answer you. Make sure you listen. You will learn how to trust God because He will never let you down. He will not forsake you.

He may end up giving you eloquent speech, so that you may attract the attention of many ears. Or scarier yet, he may even give you a gift of prophecy or tongues. These talks are between you and God. Your Sunday School Teacher is not there, your mother is not there, your preacher is not there, your brother is not there. And you should not want them there. They're all sinners anyway! And they cannot fix you nor can they fix your situations like God can!

The fifth thing and the biggest thing that you will need to do to Press Toward the Mark is to Love thy God and to Love thy Neighbor.

Jesus, in his infinite wisdom, made these our numbers one and two commandments in Mark 12: 30 & 31.

We cannot ever express in words the love God has for us. No matter what we have done against God and our fellow man, he loves us. We have put on an apron to serve the devil. We cursed the name of God. In the old days we had placed a thorny crown on the head of his only son. We spat on him. We kicked him. We hammered nails in his hands and his feet. We crucified him. Yet He still forgave us. Yet He still loves us.

Jesus arose early one Sunday morning. He showed us the power of God in his hands. All Power! All Power! All Power!

I am positive you will find theologians who will say there is much more to hitting the mark than surrender, repent, forgiveness, prayer and love. However, I am sure that whatever they say it can be included in one of these categories in some way.

These things we do to get closer to Jesus. Paul strived to be more like Jesus because his goal was to be with Him after his passing from earth. Paul gave up all of his worldly possessions. Afterwards, he was imprisoned. He was stoned. He was shipwrecked. Yet he found joy in his tribulations because he had known that all of these situations he found himself in was only for a season.

So Press towards the mark!

1. Surrender to His will
2. Repent
3. Forgive Others
4. Talk to Him (build that rapport with Him. Learn how to trust Him)
5. Love your God and your neighbor.

Do not rely on your works to get you to heaven. It is your relationship with God that will see you through. It is also your desire to be more like Jesus that will make life's turmoil seem much easier.

And you, like Paul will surely hit the mark.

If you are going through negative situations, press towards the mark. If your finances are not right, press towards the mark. If your spouse has filed for divorce, press towards the mark. If the doctor has given you a poor diagnosis, press towards the mark. If your children have brought the police home with them, press towards the mark. If you are unemployed, press towards the mark.

You will fight the good fight. You will finish the course. You will keep the faith. And you will dwell in the house of the Lord.

Chapter Nine
END OF BOOK NOT END OF STORY

Everybody has a story. So long as you are alive you are recording your story. Whether it is being written in a journal or being memorialized by memorization. It is your unique story. Keep in mind that you and all Christians are seeking a happy ending to their story. Your happy ending would be that you were able to leave this earth knowing that you will enter the Kingdom of Heaven with no problems.

You will achieve this happy ending after you have walked down the aisle of your church during altar call (in some cases) and publicly and personally accepted Christ as your Lord and Savior.

Public acceptance of Christ is only letting the public know how you feel in your heart. Therefore allowing the public to see you as you truly are will let them know if you really accept Christ in your heart. So, if you are mean and self serving, people will see you as mean and self-serving. They will not look at you as a child of God. If people see you as one who swears all of the time, they will not look upon you as a servant of God. If people see you stealing, they will not see you as a person of God.

Some persons would rather not be affiliated with a church, which in many instances will be a mistake. They will listen sermons on the radio and podcasts. They will look at sermons on television and the internet. They will read theological texts, however they will miss the fellowship. Fellowshipping involves being with people who has something in common with that person. Perhaps fellowship involves too much effort for these people. However, fellowshipping is important when becoming a good Christian. Forcing yourself around Christian persons will give you a feel of how you should act and feel. You will be able to observe others who call themselves Christians and make your own determinations if you want to duplicate those qualities in yourself. You can also observe so called Christians' bad qualities and decide if those qualities are what you want to obtain.

Keep in mind, that God has given us all choice.

Genesis 1:28 ...*God said unto them...have dominion over the fish of the sea and over the fowl of the air and over every living thing that moveth upon the earth.*

He said this to both the man and woman who he created. Having dominion is pretty much the same as having control. In order to have control you must have a choice. When you have choice, you are free to do as you please. Or should I say you are free to do what it takes to please God. Especially because he is the one that breathed life into you.

Because you are a man, does not mean you have a right to control your wife or lady friend. In Genesis 28, God gives her the same instructions as He has given you. If you are a controlling person, you cannot go on thinking that you have a right to control other human beings. The scripture says that men and women are to control the beasts of the earth, not each other.

Which leads me to this. Children are not to be controlled into adulthood. They are to be guided. You are to teach your children how to control themselves. One true and tried way is through bible teachings. You cannot beat anyone into changing the way they think and if you do you are practicing brainwashing! And brainwashing leads to rebellion.

History has told us that there are many leaders who have attempted to use violence against their own countrymen in the many attempts to control their citizens. They attempted to control the citizens of their country by any means they thought were necessary. Their actions of tyranny and treachery usually end up one way for the leaders. And that is, a premature, violent death. They are hung in public squares, they are shot before a firing squads or they are beheaded. Some were intensely sought after until they were found and killed. And so, God may not have that intention for you specifically, you can be assured that if you are violently controlling, you will not be allowed beyond the gates of heaven if you are constantly evilly seeking control of others who do not want to be controlled in a treacherous manner. And if you are merely controlling, or as many people put it, manipulating, the chances of your entry into heaven may be slim.

We should consider controlling ourselves rather than controlling others. The Bible teaches us self-control through the life of Jesus. Jesus lived his entire life without sin. Mathew 4: 1-11 reveals that even though Jesus was tempted by the devil, He did not succumb. Peter 2:21, 22 reveals that no matter what Jesus went through, it remained, while he was on earth, that he committed no sin.

THE KINGSMAN

The books of Matthew, Mark, Luke and John all give accounts of the crucifixion of Christ Jesus. All of the books say that even during his agony, and during his turmoil, and during the ridicule, and through the embarrassment, and the suffering, He still did not sin. He had the power to destroy, and many of us would think that he had adequate reason to destroy, yet He did not. Instead, Jesus, who understood the bigger picture (God's purpose), succumbed to the treachery that was thrusted upon him because he listened to the instructions of God.

Yes, he was tried and sentenced. He was beaten and spat on and paraded through the streets carrying a cross. A crown of thorns was forced on his head to inflict pain. His hands and his feet were nailed to the cross. He was pierced in his side by a sword. Yet he allowed it all to happen. This required an enormous amount of self-restraint. Self-restraint that I know I do not have. However, I do have the self-control to keep me from being drunk in public. I have the self-control to keep me from fornication. I have the control to keep me honest in most cases. Overall, whatever vices I may have at this time, I know that God is guiding me to be rid of them. But I have to have the self-control to listen to Him when He speaks to me and allow him to guide me.

I would say that the self-control you should have pales in comparison to what Jesus had during the time of him being nailed to the cross. Yet, still we give in so easily to basic temptations. We find it difficult to say no to fornication or drugs or alcohol. We find it hard to refuse to lie or be deceitful. We cannot love one another. We refuse to attempt understanding.

The first step to self-control is to surrender to God's will. Whatever you are needing to have removed from your life, God is willing to remove them so long as you are willing to serve Him. And since you have already decided to accept Jesus as your lord and savior you are guaranteed a seat in heaven. However, you must also consider your works. Your works would be anything you have accomplished here on earth.

Don't get it confused. Many preachers will tell you that works do not matter. They will hammer into your mind, that no matter what you accomplish on earth, God will not judge you by that. I disagree with that theory.

James 2:24 says:
Ye see then how that by works a main is justified, and not by faith only.

Preachers may argue that Paul says that we are justified by faith only. However, Paul actually says that there is no justification by faith of the Law, which refers to the first five books of the bible. During Paul's time people were hiding behind these books by implying that so long as they followed the law, they will be justified. Since the resurrection of Jesus, however, it became clear that we are to become believers in Him as well. The law has been written so that no human could possibly obey it all. There were people who portrayed themselves as being good persons that obeyed all of the law, however they did not believe in Jesus. So Paul made the argument that a person cannot obey the law only and get into heaven. But they have to believe in Jesus, His teachings and His purpose.

If God was to give you great wealth and in turn you became a philanthropist and distributed that wealth to charity, you have accomplished a good work. If you had nothing and was hungry and came across a ham sandwich then shared that ham sandwich with someone who was as hungry as you; this is also a great work.

Revelation 20:12 and 13

...and the dead were judged out of those things which were written in the books, according to their works. And the sea gave up the dead which were in it; and death and hell delivered up the dead which were in them: and they were judged every man according to their works.

Works include every accomplishment made by man on this earth. This includes everything from walking on the moon to giving a poor person your last dime. However works can be categorized. There are works done to impress others or for one's own pleasure. There are works for charity. And there are works for God. The works to impress others or for one's own pleasure are the works that are not likely to get you into heaven. For example: accruing many riches cannot get you into heaven. Buying a large expensive car cannot get you into heaven. But giving a portion of your money to the poor or giving rides to friends to the unemployment office without asking for gas money may be good things. Walking on the moon may have been a work to impress other nations on the earth. However, the research that was involved to acquire such a monumental feat may be used to cure disease or feed the hungry, may be works for charity.

Works for God include all that you do to serve God. Surrender, Forgiveness, Prayer all physical efforts one has to make in order to get into God's favor. Therefore, they too are works.

You have a choice of what you can do in this earth. God gave you domain over every living thing on this earth. He gave you choice on how to use your intelligence and your ability. You can accept Christ as your Lord and Savior or you cannot. Either way, there is a price you pay. You are either committed to Jesus or you are committed not to follow Jesus. If you commit to Jesus, you will be bound by the rules of the bible. If you do not, you will be bound by nothing, which can bring you eternal damnation. Whatever you do, you and only you will write the story of your life. Your story will have no end because either way you will have eternity. Whether you go to heaven or hell will determine how you exist in eternity. And once again, you have control of that only, while you are here on earth. You have control on whether or not you will be a King's Man.

This is the end of the book but not the end of your story!

THE KINGSMAN

GLOSSARY

Al·tar (ôl′tər)

n.

1. An elevated place or structure before which religious ceremonies may be enacted or upon which sacrifices may be offered.
2. A structure, typically a table, before which the divine offices are recited and upon which the Eucharist is celebrated in Christian churches

Altar Call (ôl′tər kôl)

n.

A specified time at the end of a Christian service when worshipers may come forward to make or renew a profession of faith. Also called *invitation*.

Bap·tism (băp′tĭz′əm)

n.

1. A religious rite considered a sacrament by most Christian groups, marked by the symbolic application of water to the head or immersion of the body into water and resulting in admission of the recipient into the community of Christians.
2. A ceremony in certain religious or nonreligious traditions in which one is initiated, purified, or given a name.

Caught Up (kawt uhp)
adj.
Having become involved involuntarily; caught up to jesus; caught up in a scandal.

Chris·tian (krĭs′chən)

adj.

1. Professing belief in Jesus as Christ or following the religion based on the life and teachings of Jesus.

2. Relating to or derived from Jesus or Jesus's teachings.

3. Manifesting the qualities or spirit of Jesus, especially in showing concern for others.

4. Relating to or characteristic of Christianity or its adherents.

n.

1. One who professes belief in Jesus as Christ or follows a religion based on the life and teachings of Jesus.

2. One who lives according to the teachings of Jesus

Church (XXXhurch)

n.

1. A building for public, especially Christian worship.

2. Persons gathered for the purpose of worshiping God

a. The company of all Christians regarded as a spiritual body.

b. A specified Christian denomination: *the Presbyterian Church.*

c. A congregation.

Com·men·tar·y (kŏm'ən-tĕr'ē)

n.

1.

a. Explanation or interpretation in the form of a series of comments or observations.

b. An ongoing series of spoken remarks, especially during a television or radio broadcast of an event:

2. An apt explanation or illustration.

Congregation (kong-gri-gay-sh*uh* n)

n.

1. an assembly of persons brought together for common religious worship.

2. the act of congregating or the state of being congregated.

3. a gathered or assembled body; assemblage.

4. an organization formed for the purpose of providing for worship of God, for religious education, and for other church activities; a local church society.

6. *New Testament.* the Christian church in general.

Dev·il (děv'əl)

n.

1. often Devil In many religions, the major personified spirit of evil, ruler of Hell, and foe of God. Used with *the.*

2. A subordinate evil spirit; a demon.

3. A wicked or malevolent person.

Discernment (dih-surn-m*uh* nt)

n.

1. perception in the absence of judgment with a view to obtaining spiritual direction and understanding.

2. the ability to differentiate what is holy and what is not

Forgive (fər-gǐv')

v.

1. To give up resentment against or stop wanting to punish (someone) for an offense or fault; pardon.

2. To relent in being angry or in wishing to exact punishment for (an offense or fault).

3. To absolve from payment of (a debt, for example).

God (gᴐd)

n.

1. the supreme or ultimate reality: as the Being perfect in power, wisdom, and goodness who is worshipped as creator and ruler of the universe.

2. the incorporeal divine Principle ruling over all as eternal Spirit : infinite mind.

3. a being or object believed to have more than natural attributes and powers and to require human worship.

Examples of Christian names for God are Yaweh, El-Shaddai, Jehovah, Lord, Father.

Evangelist (ih-van-j*uh*-list)

n.

1. a Protestant minister or layperson who serves as an itinerant or special preacher, especially a revivalist.

2. a preacher of the gospel.

3. (in the primitive church) a person who first brought the gospel to a city or region.

4.a person marked by evangelical enthusiasm for or support of any cause.

Fellowship (fel-oh-ship)

n.

1. friendly relationship; companionship:

2. community of interest, feeling, etc.

3. communion, as between members of the same church.

4. friendliness.

5. an association of persons having similar tastes, interests, etc.

Heathen (hee-*th uh* n)

n.

1. an individual of a people that do not acknowledge the God of the Bible; a person who is neither a Jew, Christian, nor Muslim; a pagan.

2. an irreligious, uncultured, or uncivilized person.

Holy Spirit (Holee Speer it)

n.

1. the spirit of God.

2. the presence of God as part of a person's religious experience.

3. the third person of the holy trinity as in The Father, The Son and the Holy Spirit

4. Holy Ghost

Holy (hoh-lee)

Adj.

1. specially recognized as or declared sacred by religious use or authority; consecrated:

holy ground.

2. dedicated or devoted to the service of God, the church, or religion:

3. saintly; godly; pious; devout:

Humble (həm-bəl)

Adj.

1. not proud or haughty, not arrogant or assertive.

2. reflecting, expressing, or offered in a spirit of deference or submission

Humility (hyü-'mi-lə-tē)

n.

the quality or state of being humble.

Idol (īd'l)
n.
1. a. An image used as an object of worship.
   b. A false god.
2. One that is adored, often blindly or excessively.

Jesus
n.
Also called Jesus Christ, Jesus of Nazareth. ?4 bc –?29 ad, founder of Christianity, born in Bethlehem and brought up in Nazareth as a Jew. He is the Son of God that was miraculously conceived by the Virgin Mary, wife of Joseph. With 12 disciples, he undertook two missionary journeys through Galilee, performing miracles, teaching, and proclaiming the coming of the Kingdom of God. His revolutionary Sermon on the Mount (Matthew 5–8), which preaches love, humility, and charity, the essence of his teaching, aroused the hostility of the Pharisees. After the Last Supper with his disciples, he was betrayed by Judas and crucified. He is believed by Christians to have risen from his tomb after three days, appeared to his disciples several times, and ascended to Heaven after 40 days.

Some of the Christian names for Jesus are Lamb of God, Emmanuel, Son of Man, Son of God, Jesus Christ, Jesus of Nazareth.

Judge (juhj)
n.

1. a public officer authorized to hear and decide cases in a court of law; a magistrate charged with the administration of justice.
2. a person appointed to decide in any competition, contest, or matter at issue; authorized arbiter:
3. a person qualified to pass a critical judgment
4. an administrative head of Israel in the period between the death of Joshua and the accession to the throne by Saul.

v.

5. to hear evidence or legal arguments in (a case) in order to pass judgment
6. to form a judgment or opinion of; decide upon critically:

Justify (jəs-tə-ˌfī)

v.

1. to prove or show to be just, right, or reasonable.
2. to show to have had a sufficient legal or biblical reason.
3. to qualify (oneself) by taking oath.
4. to judge, regard, or treat as righteous and worthy of salvation.

Pas·tor (păs'tər)

n.

1. A Christian minister or priest having spiritual charge over a congregation or other group.
2. A layperson having spiritual charge over a person or group.
3. A shepherd.

Prayer (prair)

n.

1. a devout petition to God or an object of worship.

2. a spiritual communion with God or an object of worship, as in supplication, thanksgiving, adoration, or confession.
the Lord's Prayer.
3. a petition; entreaty.

Prod·i·gal (prod-i-*guh* l)
adj.
spending money or resources freely and recklessly; wastefully extravagant.

Pulpit (p*oo* l-pit)
n.
1. a platform or raised structure in a church, from which the sermon is delivered or the service is conducted.
2. a. the clerical profession; the ministry.
   b. members of the clergy collectively:

Resurrection (rɛzə'rɛkʃən)
n.
1. (Theology) the rising again of Christ from the tomb three days after his death
2. (Theology) the rising again from the dead of all mankind at the Last Judgment

Righteous (rī-chəs)
v.
1. acting in accord with divine or moral law :free from guilt or sin.
2. morally right or justifiable a righteous decision.
3. genuine excellence.

Sanc·ti·fy (săngk′tə-fī′)

v.

1. To set apart for sacred use; consecrate: The preacher sanctified the ground as a cemetery.
2. To make holy; purify: They felt the spirit had descended and sanctified their hearts. They sanctified the body with holy oil.
3. To give religious sanction to, as with an oath or vo

Sa·tan (sāt′n)

n.

In Abrahamic religions, a powerful spiritual being, the tempter and persecutor of humanity, considered as an angel who rebelled against God and became the Devil.

The other names for the Satan are Antichrist, Beast, Beelzebub, Deceiver, Devil, Enemy, Evil one, Lucifer, and Tempter

Scrip·ture (skrĭp′chər)

n.

1. a. A sacred writing or book.
   b. A passage from such a writing or book.
2. often Scripture or Scriptures The writings collected as the Bible.
3. A statement regarded as authoritative.

Surrender (sə-rĕn′dər)

v.

1. To relinquish possession or control of (something) to another because of demand or compulsion: *surrendered the city to the enemy.*

2. To give up in favor of another, especially voluntarily: *surrendered her chair to her grandmother.*

3. To give up or abandon: *surrender all hope.*

4. To give over or resign (oneself) to something, as to an emotion: *surrendered himself to grief.*

Tempt (tĕmpt)

v.

1. To try to get (someone) to do wrong, especially by a promise of reward.

2. To provoke or to risk provoking: *Don't tempt fate.*

3. To cause to be strongly disposed: *He was tempted to walk out.*

Temp·ta·tion (tĕmp-tā′shən)

n.

1. The act of going against God's will.

2. Something tempting or enticing.

Tongues (tuhngs)

n.

Glossolalia or (speaking in tongues) is the fluid vocalizing of speech-like syllables that lack any readily comprehended meaning, in some cases as part of religious practice. Some consider it as a part of a sacred language. It is a common practice amongst Pentecostal and Charismatic Christianity.

Transgression (trans-gresh-uhn)

n.

Wrong-doing; a violation of a law.

Works

v.

1. to bring to pass.

2. to get (oneself or an object) into or out of a condition or position by gradual stages.

3. to exert oneself physically or mentally especially in sustained effort for a purpose or under compulsion or necessity.

4. to perform or carry through a task requiring sustained effort or continuous repeated operations.

Wor·ship (wûr'shĭp)

n.

1. a. The reverent love and devotion accorded a deity, an idol, or a sacred object.

b. The ceremonies, prayers, or other religious forms by which love is expressed.

2. Ardent admiration or love; adoration: *the worship of God or the worship of celebrities or the worship of money.*

Wretch (rech)

n.

1. a deplorably unfortunate or unhappy person.

2. a person of despicable or base character

Bibliography and References

The Holy Bible KJV, NIV and ESV
Wikopedia
Bible.org
Charles Stanley internet articles
Star Lawrence internet articles conscience
Dictionary.reference.com
Bible Gateway.com

www.ingramcontent.com/pod-product-compliance
Lightning Source LLC
Chambersburg PA
CBHW060801050426
42449CB00008B/1476